THE DOCTRINE OF REPENTANCE

The Doctrine of Repentance

THOMAS WATSON

THE BANNER OF TRUTH TRUST

THE BANNER OF TRUTH TRUST
3 Murrayfield Road, Edinburgh EH12 6EL, UK
P.O. Box 621, Carlisle, PA 17013, USA

*

First published 1668
First Banner of Truth edition 1987
Reprinted 1994
Reprinted 1999
Reprinted 2002
Reprinted 2009

ISBN-13: 978 0 85151 521 2

*

Printed in the USA by
Versa Press, Inc.
East Peoria, IL

CONTENTS

THE EPISTLE TO THE READER

CHRISTIAN READER,

The two great graces essential to a saint in this life are faith and repentance. These are the two wings by which he flies to heaven. Faith and repentance preserve the spiritual life as heat and radical moisture do the natural. The grace which I am going to discuss is repentance.

Chrysostom thought it the fittest subject for him to preach upon before the Emperor Arcadius. Augustine[1] caused the penitential psalms to be written before him as he lay upon his bed, and he often perused them with tears. Repentance is never out of season; it is of as frequent use as the artificer's tool or the soldier's weapon. If I am not mistaken, practical points are more needful in this age than controversial and polemical.

I had thought to have smothered these meditations in my desk but, conceiving them to be of great concern at this juncture of time, I have rescinded my first resolution and have exposed them to a critical view.

Repentance is purgative; fear not the working of this pill. Smite your soul, said Chrysostom, smite it; it will escape death by that stroke. How happy it would be if we were more deeply affected with sin, and our eyes did swim in their orb. We may clearly see the Spirit of God moving in the waters of repentance, which though troubled, are yet pure. Moist tears dry up sin and quench the wrath of God. Repentance is the cherisher of piety, the procurer of mercy. The more regret and trouble of spirit we have first at our conversion, the less we shall feel afterwards.

Christians, do you have a sad resentment of other

---

[1] One of the greatest of the Church Fathers; he died in 430. Watson calls him Austin.

things and not of sin? Worldly tears fall to the earth, but godly tears are kept in a bottle (*Ps. 56.8*). Judge not holy weeping superfluous. Tertullian thought he was born for no other end but to repent. Either sin must drown or the soul burn. Let it not be said that repentance is difficult. Things that are excellent deserve labour. Will not a man dig for gold in the ore though it makes him sweat? It is better to go with difficulty to heaven than with ease to hell. What would the damned give that they might have a herald sent to them from God to proclaim mercy upon their repentance? What vollies of sighs and groans would they send up to heaven? What floods of tears would their eyes pour forth? But it is now too late. They may keep their tears to lament their folly sooner than to procure pity. O that we would therefore, while we are on this side of the grave, make our peace with God! Tomorrow may be our dying day; let this be our repenting day. How we should imitate the saints of old who embittered their souls and sacrificed their lusts, and put on sackcloth in the hope of white robes. Peter baptized himself with tears; and that devout lady Paula (of whom Jerome writes), like a bird of paradise, bemoaned herself and humbled herself to the dust for sin.

Besides our own personal miscarriages, the deplorable condition of the land calls for a contribution of tears. Have we not lost much of our pristine fame and renown? The time was when we sat as princess among the provinces (*Lam. 1.1*), and God made the sheaves of other nations do obeisance to our sheaf (*Gen. 37.7*), but has not our glory fled away as a bird (*Hos. 9.11*)? And what severe dispensations are yet behind we cannot tell. Our black and hideous vapours having ascended, we may fear loud thunder-claps should follow. And will not all this bring us to our senses and excite in us a spirit of humiliation? Shall we sleep on the top of the mast when the winds are blowing from all the quarters of heaven? O let not the apple of our eye cease (*Lam. 2.18*)!

I will not launch forth any further in a prefatory discourse, but that God would add a blessing to this work and so direct this arrow, that though shot at rovers, it may hit the mark, and that some sin may be shot to death, shall be the ardent prayer of him who is

The well-wisher of your soul's happiness,
THOMAS WATSON

25 May 1668

Chapter One

A PRELIMINARY DISCOURSE

Saint Paul, having been falsely accused of sedition by Tertullus – 'we have found this man a pestilent fellow, and a mover of sedition' (*Acts* 24.5) – makes an apology for himself before Festus and King Agrippa in Chapter 26 of the Book of Acts.

Paul proves himself an orator. He courts the king (1) by his gesture: he stretched forth his hands, as was the custom of orators; (2) by his manner of speech: 'I think myself happy, king Agrippa, because I shall answer for myself before thee touching all the things whereof I am accused' (*Acts* 26.2).

Paul then treats of three things and in so deep a strain of rhetoric as almost to have converted King Agrippa:

(1) He speaks of the manner of his life before his conversion: 'after the most straitest sect of our religion I lived a Pharisee' (*v.5*). During the time of his unregeneracy he was zealous for traditions, and his false fire of zeal was so hot that it scorched all who stood in his way; 'many of the saints did I shut up in prison' (*v.10*).

(2) He speaks of the manner of his conversion: 'I saw in the way a light from heaven, above the brightness of the sun' (*v.13*). This light was no other than what shone from Christ's glorified body. 'And I heard a voice speaking unto me, Saul, Saul, why persecutest thou me?' The body being hurt, the head in heaven cried out. At this light and voice Paul was amazed and fell to the earth: 'And I said, Who art thou, Lord? And he said, I am Jesus

whom thou persecutest' (*vv. 14–15*). Paul was now taken off from himself. All opinion of self-righteousness vanished and he grafted his hope of heaven upon the stock of Christ's righteousness.

(3) He speaks of the manner of his life after his conversion. He who had been a persecutor before now became a preacher: 'Arise, for I have appeared unto thee for this purpose, to make thee a minister and a witness of those things which thou hast seen' (*v. 16*). When Paul, this 'vessel of election', was savingly wrought upon, he laboured to do as much good as previously he had done hurt. He had persecuted saints to death before, now he preached sinners to life. God first sent him to the Jews at Damascus and afterwards enlarged his commission to preach to the Gentiles. And the subject he preached on was this, 'That they should repent and turn to God, and do works meet for repentance' (*v. 20*). A weighty and excellent subject!

I shall not dispute the priority, whether faith or repentance goes first. Doubtless repentance shows itself first in a Christian's life. Yet I am apt to think that the seeds of faith are first wrought in the heart. As when a burning taper is brought into a room the light shows itself first, but the taper was before the light, so we see the fruits of repentance first, but the beginnings of faith were there before.

That which inclines me to think that faith is seminally in the heart before repentance is because repentance, being a grace, must be exercised by one that is living. Now, how does the soul live but by faith? 'The just shall live by his faith' (*Heb. 10.38*). Therefore there must be first some seeds of faith in the heart of a penitent, otherwise it is a dead repentance and so of no value.

Whether faith or repentance goes first, however, I am sure that repentance is of such importance that there is no being saved without it. After Paul's shipwreck he swam to shore on planks and broken pieces of the ship (*Acts* 27.44). In Adam we all suffered shipwreck, and repentance is the only plank left us after shipwreck to swim to heaven.

It is a great duty incumbent upon Christians solemnly to repent and turn unto God: 'Repent ye, for the kingdom of heaven is at hand' (*Matt.* 3.2); 'Repent therefore, and be converted that your sins may be blotted out' (*Acts* 3.19); 'Repent of this thy wickedness' (*Acts* 8.22). In the mouths of three witnesses this truth is confirmed. Repentance is a foundation grace: 'Not laying again the foundation of repentance' (*Heb.* 6.1). That religion which is not built upon this foundation must needs fall to the ground.

Repentance is a grace required under the gospel. Some think it legal; but the first sermon that Christ preached, indeed, the first word of his sermon, was 'Repent' (*Matt.* 4.17). And his farewell that he left when he was going to ascend was that 'repentance should be preached in his name' (*Luke* 24.47). The apostles did all beat upon this string: 'They went out and preached that men should repent' (*Mark* 6.12).

Repentance is a pure gospel grace. The covenant of works admitted no repentance; there it was, sin and die. Repentance came in by the gospel. Christ has purchased in his blood that repenting sinners shall be saved. The law required personal, perfect, and perpetual obedience. It cursed all who could not come up to this: 'Cursed is everyone that continueth not in all things which are written in the book of the law to do them' (*Gal.* 3.10). It does not say, he that obeys not all things, let him repent, but, let him be cursed. Thus repentance is a doctrine that has been brought to light only by the gospel.

How is repentance wrought? The manner in which repentance is wrought is:

1. *Partly by the word*

'When they heard this, they were pricked in their heart' (*Acts* 2.37). The word preached is the engine God uses to effect repentance. It is compared to a hammer and to a fire (*Jer.* 23.29), the one to break, the other to melt the heart. How great a blessing it is to have the word, which is of such virtue, dispensed! And how hard they who put out the lights of heaven will find it to escape hell!

2. *By the Spirit*

Ministers are but the pipes and organs. It is the Holy Ghost breathing in them that makes their words effectual: 'While Peter yet spake these words, the Holy Ghost fell on all them which heard the word' (*Acts* 10.44). The Spirit in the word illuminates and converts. When the Spirit touches a heart it dissolves with tears: 'I will pour upon the inhabitants of Jerusalem the spirit of grace . . . and they shall look upon me whom they have pierced, and they shall mourn' (*Zech.* 12.10). It is wonderful to consider what different effects the word has upon men. Some at a sermon are like Jonah: their heart is tender and they let fall tears. Others are no more affected with it than a deaf man with music. Some grow better by the word, others worse. The same earth which causes sweetness in the grape causes bitterness in the wormwood. What is the reason the word works so differently? It is because the Spirit of God carries the word to the conscience of one and not another. One has received the divine unction and not the other (*1 John* 2.20). O pray that the dew may fall with the manna, that the Spirit may go along with the word. The chariot of ordinances will not carry us to heaven unless the Spirit of God join himself to this chariot (*Acts* 8.29).

Chapter Two

COUNTERFEIT REPENTANCE

To discover what true repentance is, I shall first show what it is not. There are several deceits of repentance which might occasion that saying of Augustine that 'repentance damns many'. He meant a false repentance; a person may delude himself with counterfeit repentance.

1. *The first deceit of repentance is legal terror*

A man has gone on long in sin. At last God arrests him, shows him what desperate hazard he has run, and he is filled with anguish. Within a while the tempest of conscience is blown over, and he is quiet. Then he concludes that he is a true penitent because he has felt some bitterness in sin. Do not be deceived: this is not repentance. Ahab and Judas had some trouble of mind. It is one thing to be a terrified sinner and another to be a repenting sinner. Sense of guilt is enough to breed terror. Infusion of grace breeds repentance. If pain and trouble were sufficient to repentance, then the damned in hell should be most penitent, for they are most in anguish. Repentance depends upon a change of heart. There may be terror, yet with no change of heart.

2. *Another deceit about repentance is resolution against sin*

A person may purpose and make vows, yet be no penitent. 'Thou saidst, I will not transgress' (*Jer.* 2.20). Here was a resolution; but see what follows: 'under every green tree thou wanderest, playing the harlot'. Notwithstanding her solemn engagements, she played fast and loose with God and ran after her idols. We see by experience what protestations a person will make when he is on his sick-bed, if God should recover him again; yet he is as bad as ever. He shows his old heart in a new temptation.

Resolutions against sin may arise:

(1) From present extremity; not because sin is sinful, but because it is painful. This resolution will vanish.

(2) From fear of future evil, an apprehension of death and hell: 'I looked, and behold a pale horse: and his name that sat on him was Death, and Hell followed with him' (*Rev. 6.8*). What will not a sinner do, what vows will he not make, when he knows he must die and stand before the judgment-seat? Self-love raises a sick-bed vow, and love of sin will prevail against it. Trust not to a passionate resolution; it is raised in a storm and will die in a calm.

3. *The third deceit about repentance is the leaving of many sinful ways*

It is a great matter, I confess, to leave sin. So dear is sin to a man that he will rather part with a child than with a lust: 'Shall I give the fruit of my body for the sin of my soul?' (*Mic. 6.7*). Sin may be parted with, yet without repentance.

(1) A man may part with some sins and keep others, as Herod reformed many things that were amiss but could not leave his incest.

(2) An old sin may be left in order to entertain a new, as you put off an old servant to take another. This is to exchange a sin. Sin may be exchanged and the heart remained unchanged. He who was a prodigal in his youth turns usurer in his old age. A slave is sold to a Jew; the Jew sells him to a Turk. Here the master is changed, but he is a slave still. So a man moves from one vice to another but remains a sinner still.

(3) A sin may be left not so much from strength of grace as from reasons of prudence. A man sees that though such a sin be for his pleasure, yet it is not for his interest. It will eclipse his credit, prejudice his health, impair his estate. Therefore, for prudential reasons, he dismisses it.

True leaving of sin is when the acts of sin cease from the infusion of a principle of grace, as the air ceases to be dark from the infusion of light.

Chapter Three

THE NATURE OF TRUE REPENTANCE (1)

I shall next show what gospel repentance is. Repentance is a grace of God's Spirit whereby a sinner is inwardly humbled and visibly reformed. For a further amplification, know that repentance is a spiritual medicine made up of six special ingredients:

1. Sight of sin
2. Sorrow for sin
3. Confession of sin
4. Shame for sin
5. Hatred for sin
6. Turning from sin

If any one is left out it loses its virtue.

Ingredient 1: Sight of Sin

The first part of Christ's physic is eye-salve (*Acts 26.18*). It is the great thing noted in the prodigal's repentance: 'he came to himself' (*Luke 15.17*). He saw himself a sinner and nothing but a sinner. Before a man can come to Christ he must first come to himself. Solomon, in his description of repentance, considers this as the first ingredient: 'if they shall bethink themselves' (*1 Kings 8.47*). A man must first recognize and consider what his sin is, and know the plague of his heart before he can be duly humbled for it. The first creature God made was light. So the first thing in a penitent is illumination: 'Now ye are light in the Lord' (*Eph. 5.8*). The eye is made

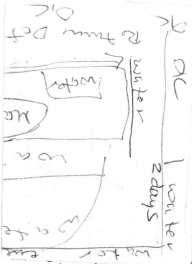

. Sin must first be seen before

...ere is no sight of sin, there can
...o can spy faults in others see
...y that they have good hearts. Is
...uld live together, and eat and
...v each other? Such is the case of
...l live together, work together,
...himself. He knows not his own
...rries about him. Under a veil a
...ersons are veiled over with
...therefore they see not what
deformed souls they have. The devil does with them as the
falconer with the hawk. He blinds them and carries them
hooded to hell: 'the sword shall be upon his right eye'
(*Zech. 11.17*). Men have insight enough into worldly
matters, but the eye of their mind is smitten. They do not
see any evil in sin; the sword is upon their right eye.

Ingredient 2: Sorrow for Sin
I will be sorry for my sin (Psalm 38.18)

Ambrose calls sorrow the embittering of the soul. The
Hebrew word 'to be sorrowful' signifies 'to have the soul,
as it were, crucified'. This must be in true repentance:
'They shall look upon me whom they have pierced, and
they shall mourn' (*Zech. 12.10*), as if they did feel the
nails of the cross sticking in their sides. A woman may as
well expect to have a child without pangs as one can have
repentance without sorrow. He that can believe without
doubting, suspect his faith; and he that can repent
without sorrowing, suspect his repentance.

Martyrs shed blood for Christ, and penitents shed
tears for sin: 'she stood at Jesus' feet weeping' (*Luke
7.38*). See how this limbeck[1] dropped. The sorrow of her

---

[1] i.e. alembic: old distilling apparatus (for refining liquids).

heart ran out at her eye. The brazen laver for the priests to wash in (*Exod. 30.18*) typified a double laver: the laver of Christ's blood we must wash in by faith, and the laver of tears we must wash in by repentance. A true penitent labours to work his heart into a sorrowing frame. He blesses God when he can weep; he is glad of a rainy day, for he knows that it is a repentance he will have no cause to repent of. Though the bread of sorrow be bitter to the taste, yet it strengthens the heart (*Ps. 104.15; 2 Cor. 7.10*).

This sorrow for sin is not superficial: it is a holy agony. It is called in scripture a breaking of the heart: 'The sacrifices of God are a broken and a contrite heart' (*Ps. 51.17*); and a rending of the heart: 'Rend your heart' (*Joel 2.13*). The expressions of smiting on the thigh (*Jer. 31.19*), beating on the breast (*Luke 18.13*), putting on of sackcloth (*Isa. 22.12*), plucking off the hair (*Ezra 9.3*), all these are but outward signs of inward sorrow. This sorrow is:

(1) To make Christ precious. O how desirable is a Saviour to a troubled soul! Now Christ is Christ indeed, and mercy is mercy indeed. Until the heart is full of compunction it is not fit for Christ. How welcome is a surgeon to a man who is bleeding from his wounds!

(2) To drive out sin. Sin breeds sorrow, and sorrow kills sin. Holy sorrow is the rhubarb to purge out the ill humours of the soul. It is said that the tears of vine-branches are good to cure the leprosy. Certainly the tears that drop from the penitent are good to cure the leprosy of sin. The salt water of tears kills the worm of conscience.

(3) To make way for solid comfort: 'They that sow in tears shall reap in joy' (*Ps. 126.5*). The penitent has a wet seed-time but a delicious harvest. Repentance breaks the abscess of sin, and then the soul is at ease. Hannah, after

weeping, went away and was no more sad (*1 Sam. 1.18*). God's troubling of the soul for sin is like the angel's troubling of the pool (*John 5.4*), which made way for healing.

But not all sorrow evidences true repentance. There is as much difference between true and false sorrow as between water in the spring, which is sweet, and water in the sea, which is briny. The apostle speaks of sorrowing 'after a godly manner' (*2 Cor. 7.9*). But what is this godly sorrowing? There are six qualifications of it:

1. *True godly sorrow is inward*

It is inward in two ways:

(1) It is a sorrow of the heart. The sorrow of hypocrites lies in their faces: 'they disfigure their faces' (*Matt. 6.16*). They make a sour face, but their sorrow goes no further, like the dew that wets the leaf but does not soak to the root. Ahab's repentance was in outward show. His garments were rent but not his spirit (*1 Kings 21.27*). Godly sorrow goes deep, like a vein which bleeds inwardly. The heart bleeds for sin: 'they were pricked in their heart' (*Acts 2.37*). As the heart bears a chief part in sinning, so it must in sorrowing.

(2) It is a sorrow for heart-sins, the first outbreaks and risings of sin. Paul grieved for the law in his members (*Rom. 7.23*). The true mourner weeps for the stirrings of pride and concupiscence. He grieves for the 'root of bitterness' even though it never blossoms into act. A wicked man may be troubled for scandalous sins; a real convert laments heart-sins.

2. *Godly sorrow is ingenuous*

It is sorrow for the offence rather than for the punishment. God's law has been infringed, his love abused. This melts the soul in tears. A man may be sorry, yet not repent, as a thief is sorry when he is taken, not because he stole, but because he has to pay the penalty. Hypocrites grieve only for the bitter consequence of sin. I have read of a fountain that only sends forth streams on the evening before a famine. Likewise their eyes never pour out tears except when God's judgments are approaching. Pharaoh was more troubled for the frogs and river of blood than for his sin. Godly sorrow, however, is chiefly for the trespass against God, so that even if there were no conscience to smite, no devil to accuse, no hell to punish, yet the soul would still be grieved because of the prejudice done to God. 'My sin is ever before me' (*Ps. 51.3*); David does not say, The sword threatened is ever before me, but 'my sin'. O that I should offend so good a God, that I should grieve my Comforter! This breaks my heart!

Godly sorrow shows itself to be ingenuous because when a Christian knows that he is out of the gun-shot of hell and shall never be damned, yet still he grieves for sinning against that free grace which has pardoned him.

3. *Godly sorrow is fiducial*[1]

It is intermixed with faith: 'the father of the child cried out, and said with tears, Lord, I believe' (*Mark 9.24*). Here was sorrow for sin chequered with faith, as we have seen a bright rainbow appear in a watery cloud.

Spiritual sorrow will sink the heart if the pulley of faith does not raise it. As our sin is ever before us, so God's promise must be ever before us. As we much feel our sting, so we must look up to Christ our brazen serpent. Some have faces so swollen with worldly grief that they can hardly look out of their eyes. That weeping is not good which blinds the eye of faith. If there are not some dawnings of faith in the soul, it is not the sorrow of humiliation but of despair.

4. *Godly sorrow is a great sorrow*

'In that day shall there be a great mourning, as the

---

[1]Trustful.

mourning of Hadadrimmon' (*Zech.* 12.11). Two suns did set that day when Josiah died, and there was a great funeral mourning. To such a height must sorrow for sin be boiled up. *Pectore ab imo suspiria.*[1]

Question 1: Do all have the same degree of sorrow?

Answer: No, sorrow does *recipere magis & minus* (produce greater or lesser [sorrows]). In the new birth all have pangs, but some have sharper pangs than others.

(1) Some are naturally of a more rugged disposition, of higher spirits, and are not easily brought to stoop. These must have greater humiliation, as a knotty piece of timber must have greater wedges driven into it.

(2) Some have been more heinous offenders, and their sorrow must be suitable to their sin. Some patients have their sores let out with a needle, others with a lance. Flagitious[2] sinners must be more bruised with the hammer of the law.

(3) Some are designed and cut out for higher service, to be eminently instrumental for God, and these must have a mightier work of humiliation pass upon them. Those whom God intends to be pillars in his church must be more hewn. Paul, the prince of the apostles, who was to be God's ensign-bearer to carry his name before the Gentiles and kings, was to have his heart more deeply lanced by repentance.

Question 2: But how great must sorrow for sin be in all?

Answer: It must be as great as for any worldly loss. *Turgescunt lumina fletu.*[3] 'They shall look upon me whom they have pierced, and they shall mourn as for an only son' (*Zech.* 12.10). Sorrow for sin must surpass worldly sorrow. We must grieve more for

[1]'Sighings from the bottom of one's heart.'
[2]Extremely wicked (sinners).
[3]'Eyes are swollen with weeping.'

offending God than for the loss of dear relations. 'In that day did the Lord God of hosts call to weeping, and to baldness, and to girding with sackcloth' (*Isa. 22.12*): this was for sin. But in the case of the burial of the dead we find God prohibiting tears and baldness (*Jer. 22.10; 16.6*), to intimate that sorrow for sin must exceed sorrow at the grave; and with good reason, for in the burial of the dead it is only a friend who departs, but in sin God departs.

Sorrow for sin should be so great as to swallow up all other sorrow, as when the pain of the stone and gout meet, the pain of the stone swallows up the pain of the gout.

We are to find as much bitterness in weeping for sin as ever we found sweetness in committing it. Surely David found more bitterness in repentance than ever he found comfort in Bathsheba.

Our sorrow for sin must be such as makes us willing to let go of those sins which brought in the greatest income of profit or delight. The physic shows itself strong enough when it has purged out our disease. The Christian has arrived at a sufficient measure of sorrow when the love of sin is purged out.

5. *Godly sorrow in some cases is joined with restitution*
Whoever has wronged others in their estate by unjust fraudulent dealing ought in conscience to make them recompense. There is an express law for this: 'he shall recompense his trespass with the principal thereof, and add unto it the fifth part thereof, and give it unto him against whom he hath trespassed' (*Num. 5.7*). Thus Zacchæus made restitution: 'if I have taken any thing from any man by false accusation, I restore him fourfold' (*Luke 19.8*). When Selymus the great Turk, lay upon his death-bed, being urged by Pyrrhus to put to charitable use that wealth he had wronged the Persian merchants of,

he commanded rather that it should be sent back to the right owners. Shall not a Christian's creed be better than a Turk's Koran? It is a bad sign when a man on his death-bed bequeaths his soul to God and his ill-gotten goods to his friends. I can hardly think God will receive his soul. Augustine said, 'Without restitution, no remission'. And it was a speech of old Latimer, If ye restore not goods unjustly gotten, ye shall cough in hell.

Question 1: Suppose a person has wronged another in his estate and the wronged man is dead, what should he do?

Answer: Let him restore his ill-gotten goods to that man's heirs and successors. If none of them be living, let him restore to God, that is, let him put his unjust gain into God's treasury by relieving the poor.

Question 2: What if the party who did the wrong is dead?

Answer: Then they who are his heirs ought to make restitution. Mark what I say: if there be any who have estates left them, and they know that the parties who left their estates had defrauded others and died with that guilt upon them, then the heirs or executors who possess those estates are bound in conscience to make restitution, otherwise they entail the curse of God upon their family.

Question 3: If a man has wronged another and is not able to restore, what should he do?

Answer: Let him deeply humble himself before God, promising to the wronged party full satisfaction if the Lord make him able, and God will accept the will for the deed.

6. *Godly sorrow is abiding*

It is not a few tears shed in a passion that will serve the turn. Some will fall a-weeping at a sermon, but it is like an April shower, soon over, or like a vein opened and presently stopped again. True sorrow must be habitual.

O Christian, the disease of your soul is chronic and frequently returns upon you; therefore you must be continually physicking yourself by repentance. This is that sorrow which is 'after a godly manner'.

Use: How far are they from repentance who never had any of this godly sorrow! Such are:

(1) The Papists, who leave out the very soul of repentance, making all penitential work consist in fasting, penance, pilgrimages, in which there is nothing of spiritual sorrow. They torture their bodies, but their hearts are not rent. What is this but the carcase of repentance?

(2) Carnal Protestants, who are strangers to godly sorrow. They cannot endure a serious thought, nor do they love to trouble their heads about sin. Paracelsus[1] spoke of a frenzy some have which will make them die dancing. Likewise sinners spend their days in mirth; they fling away sorrow and go dancing to damnation. Some have lived many years, yet never put a drop in God's bottle, nor do they know what a broken heart means. They weep and wring their hands as if they were undone when their estates are gone, but have no agony of soul for sin.

There is a two-fold sorrow: firstly, a rational sorrow, which is an act of the soul whereby it has a displacency against sin and chooses any torture rather than to admit sin; secondly, there is a sensitive sorrow, which is expressed by many tears. The first of these is to be found in every child of God, but the second, which is a sorrow running out at the eye, all have not. Yet it is very commendable to see a weeping penitent. Christ counts as great beauties those who are tender-eyed; and well may sin make us weep. We usually weep for the loss of some

[1] A Swiss physician (16th century).

great good; by sin we have lost the favour of God. If Micah did so weep for the loss of a false god, saying, 'Ye have taken away my gods, and what have I more?' (*Judges 18.24*) then well may we weep for our sins which have taken away the true God from us.

Some may ask the question, whether our repentance and sorrow must always be alike. Although repentance must be always kept alive in the soul, yet there are two special times when we must renew our repentance in an extraordinary manner:

(1) Before the receiving of the Lord's Supper. This spiritual passover is to be eaten with bitter herbs. Now our eyes should be fresh broached with tears, and the stream of sorrow overflow. A repenting frame is a sacramental frame. A broken heart and a broken Christ do well agree. The more bitterness we taste in sin, the more sweetness we shall taste in Christ. When Jacob wept he found God: 'And he called the name of the place Peniel: for I have seen God face to face' (*Gen. 32.30*). The way to find Christ comfortably in the sacrament is to go weeping thither. Christ will say to a humble penitent, as to Thomas: 'Reach hither thy hand, and thrust it into my side' (*John 20.27*), and let those bleeding wounds of mine heal thee.

(2) Another time of extraordinary repentance is at the hour of death. This should be a weeping season. Now is our last work to be done for heaven, and our best wine of tears should be kept against such a time. We should repent now, that we have sinned so much and wept so little, that God's bag has been so full and his bottle so empty (*Job 14.17*). We should repent now that we repented no sooner, that the garrisons of our hearts held out so long against God ere they were levelled by repentance. We should repent now that we have loved

Christ no more, that we have fetched no more virtue from him and brought no more glory to him. It should be our grief on our death-bed that our lives have had so many blanks and blots in them, that our duties have been so fly-blown with sin, that our obedience has been so imperfect, and we have gone so lame in the ways of God. When the soul is going out of the body, it should swim to heaven in a sea of tears.

Ingredient 3: Confession of Sin

Sorrow is such a vehement passion that it will have vent. It vents itself at the eyes by weeping and at the tongue by confession: 'The children of Israel stood and confessed their sins (*Neh.* 9.2). 'I will go and return to my place, till they acknowledge their offence' (*Hos.* 5.15); it is a metaphor alluding to a mother who, when she is angry, goes away from the child and hides her face till the child acknowledges its fault and begs pardon. Gregory Nazianzen[1] calls confession 'a salve for a wounded soul.'

Confession is self-accusing: 'Lo, I have sinned' (2 *Sam.* 24.17). Indeed, among men it is otherwise: no man is bound to accuse himself but desires to see his accuser. When we come before God, however, we must accuse ourselves: *me me adsum qui feci in me convertite ferrum.*[2] And the truth is that by this self-accusing we prevent Satan's accusing. In our confessions we tax ourselves with pride, infidelity, passion, so that when Satan, who is called 'the accuser of the brethren', shall lay these things to our charge, God will say, They have accused themselves already; therefore, Satan, thou art non-suited; thy accusations come too late. The humble sinner does more

---

[1] A fourth century defender of the faith.
[2] '[O Lord] I, even I, who made myself what I am, change my hardness [of heart].'

than accuse himself; he, as it were, sits in judgment and passes sentence upon himself. He confesses that he has deserved to be bound over to the wrath of God. And hear what the apostle Paul says: 'if we would judge ourselves we should not be judged' (*1 Cor. 11.31*).

But have not wicked men, like Judas and Saul, confessed sin? Yes, but theirs was not a true confession. That confession of sin may be right and genuine, these eight qualifications are requisite:

1. *Confession must be voluntary*

It must come as water out of a spring, freely. The confession of the wicked is extorted, like the confession of a man upon a rack. When a spark of God's wrath flies into their conscience, or they are in fear of death, then they will fall to their confessions. Balaam, when he saw the angel's naked sword, could say, 'I have sinned' (*Num. 22.34*). But true confession drops from the lips as myrrh from the tree or honey from the comb, freely. 'I have sinned against heaven, and before thee' (*Luke 15.18*): the prodigal charged himself with sin before his father charged him with it.

2. *Confession must be with compunction*

The heart must deeply resent it. A natural man's confessions run through him as water through a pipe. They do not at all affect him. But true confession leaves heart-wounding impressions on a man. David's soul was burdened in the confession of his sins: 'as an heavy burden they are too heavy for me' (*Ps. 38.4*). It is one thing to confess sin and another thing to feel sin.

3. *Confession must be sincere*

Our hearts must go along with our confessions. The hypocrite confesses sin but loves it, like a thief who confesses to stolen goods, yet loves stealing. How many confess pride and covetousness with their lips but roll them as honey under their tongue. Augustine said that

[29]

before his conversion he confessed sin and begged power against it, but his heart whispered within him, 'not yet, Lord'. He was afraid to leave his sin too soon. A good Christian is more honest. His heart keeps pace with his tongue. He is convinced of the sins he confesses, and abhors the sins he is convinced of.

4. *In true confession a man particularizes sin*
A wicked man acknowledges he is a sinner in general. He confesses sin by wholesale. His confession of sin is much like Nebuchadnezzar's dream: 'I have dreamed a dream' (*Dan. 2.3*), but he could not tell what it was: 'The thing is gone from me' (*Dan. 2.5*). In the same way a wicked man says, 'Lord, I have sinned', but does not know what the sin is; at least he does not remember, whereas a true convert acknowledges his particular sins. As it is with a wounded man, who comes to the surgeon and shows him all his wounds – here I was cut in the head, there I was shot in the arm – so a mournful sinner confesses the several distempers of his soul. Israel drew up a particular charge against themselves: 'we have served Baalim' (*Judg. 10.10*). The prophet recites the very sin which brought a curse with it: 'Neither have we hearkened unto thy servants the prophets, which spake in thy name' (*Dan. 9.6*). By a diligent inspection into our hearts we may find some particular sin indulged; point to that sin with a tear.

5. *A true penitent confesses sin in the fountain*
He acknowledges the pollution of his nature. The sin of our nature is not only a privation of good but an infusion of evil. It is like canker to iron or stain to scarlet. David acknowledges his birth-sin: 'I was shapen in iniquity; and in sin did my mother conceive me' (*Ps. 51.5*). We are ready to charge many of our first sins to Satan's temptations, but this sin of our nature is wholly from ourselves; we cannot shift it off to Satan. We have a root

within that bears gall and wormwood (*Deut. 29.18*). Our nature is an abyss and seminary of all evil, from whence come those scandals that infest the world. It is this depravity of nature which poisons our holy things; it is this which brings on God's judgments and makes our mercies stick in the birth. Oh confess sin in the fountain!

6. *Sin is to be confessed with all its circumstances and aggravations*

Those sins which are committed under the gospel horizon are doubtless dyed in grain. Confess sins against knowledge, against grace, against vows, against experiences, against judgments. 'The wrath of God came upon them and slew the fattest of them. For all this they sinned still' (*Ps. 78.31–2*). These are killing aggravations which do accent and enhance our sins.

7. *In confession we must so charge ourselves as to clear God*

Should the Lord be severe in his providences and unsheath his bloody sword, yet we must acquit him and acknowledge he has done us no wrong. Nehemiah in his confessing of sin vindicates God's righteousness: 'Howbeit thou art just in all that is brought upon us' (*Neh. 9.33*). Mauritius[1] the emperor, when he saw his wife slain before his eyes by Phocas, cried out, 'Righteous art thou, O Lord, in all thy ways'.

8. *We must confess our sins with a resolution not to act them over again*

Some run from the confessing of sin to the committing of sin, like the Persians who have one day in the year when they kill serpents and after that day suffer them to swarm again. Likewise, many seem to kill their sins in their confessions and afterwards let them grow as fast as ever. 'Cease to do evil' (*Isa. 1.16*). It is vain to confess, 'We

---

[1] Roman emperor (582–602). Phocas became emperor after Mauritius.

have done those things we ought not to have done', and continue still in doing so. Pharaoh confessed he had sinned (*Exod. 9.27*), but when the thunder ceased he fell to his sin again: 'he sinned yet more, and hardened his heart' (*Exod. 9.34*). Origen[1] calls confession the vomit of the soul whereby the conscience is eased of that burden which did lie upon it. Now, when we have vomited up sin by confession we must not return to this vomit. What king will pardon that man who, after he has confessed his treason, practises new treason?

Thus we see how confession must be qualified.

Use 1: Is confession a necessary ingredient in repentance? Here is a bill of indictment against four sorts of persons:

(1) It reproves those that hide their sins, as Rachel hid her father's images under her (*Gen. 31.34*). Many had rather have their sins covered than cured. They do with their sins as with their pictures: they draw a curtain over them; or as some do with their bastards, smother them. But though men will have no tongue to confess, God has an eye to see; he will unmask their treason: 'I will reprove thee, and set them in order before thine eyes' (*Ps. 50.21*). Those iniquities which men hide in their hearts shall be written one day on their foreheads as with the point of a diamond. They who will not confess their sin as David did, that they may be pardoned, shall confess their sin as Achan did, that they may be stoned. It is dangerous to keep the devil's counsel: 'He that covereth his sins shall not prosper' (*Prov. 28.13*).

(2) It reproves those who do indeed confess sin but only by halves. They do not confess all; they confess the pence but not the pounds. They confess vain thoughts or badness of memory but not the sins they are most guilty

---

[1]One of the early Greek Fathers; he died in 254.

of, such as rash anger, extortion, uncleanness, like he in Plutarch who complained his stomach was not very good when his lungs were bad and his liver rotten. But if we do not confess all, how should we expect that God will pardon all? It is true that we cannot know the exact catalogue of our sins, but the sins which come within our view and cognizance, and which our hearts accuse us of, must be confessed as ever we hope for mercy.

(3) It reproves those who in their confessions mince and extenuate their sins. A gracious soul labours to make the worst of his sins, but hypocrites make the best of them. They do not deny they are sinners, but they do what they can to lessen their sins: they indeed offend sometimes, but it is their nature, and it is long of such occasions. These are excuses rather than confessions. 'I have sinned: for I have transgressed the commandment of the Lord: because I feared the people' (*1 Sam.* 15.24). Saul lays his sin upon the people: they would have him spare the sheep and oxen. It was an apology, not a self-indictment. This runs in the blood. Adam acknowledged that he had tasted the forbidden fruit, but instead of aggravating his sin he translated[1] it from himself to God: 'The woman thou gavest to be with me, she gave me of the tree and I did eat' (*Gen.* 3.12), that is, if I had not had this woman to be a tempter, I would not have transgressed. *Inscripsere deos sceleri*[2] (Ovid). That is a bad sin indeed that has no excuse, as it must be a very coarse wool which will take no dye. How apt we are to pare and curtail sin, and look upon it through the small end of the perspective,[3] that it appears but as 'a little cloud, like a man's hand' (*1 Kings* 18.44).

[1] Removed.
[2] 'They charge the gods with the crime.'
[3] Telescope or microscope.

(4) It reproves those who are so far from confessing sin that they boldly plead for it. Instead of having tears to lament it, they use arguments to defend it. If their sin be passion they will justify it: 'I do well to be angry' (*Jon. 4.9*). If it be covetousness they will vindicate it. When men commit sin they are the devil's servants; when they plead for it they are the devil's attorneys, and he will give them a fee.

Use 2: Let us show ourselves penitents by sincere confession of sin. The thief on the cross made a confession of his sin: 'we indeed are condemned justly' (*Luke 23.41*). And Christ said to him, 'Today shalt thou be with me in paradise' (*Luke 23.43*), which might have occasioned that speech of Augustine's, that confession of sin shuts the mouth of hell and opens the gate of paradise. That we may make a free and ingenuous confession of sin, let us consider:

(1) Holy confession gives glory to God: 'My son, give, I pray thee, glory to the Lord God of Israel, and make confession unto him' (*Josh. 7.19*). A humble confession exalts God. What a glory is it to him that out of our own mouths he does not condemn us? While we confess sin, God's patience is magnified in sparing, and his free grace in saving such sinners.

(2) Confession is a means to humble the soul. He who subscribes himself a hell-deserving sinner will have little heart to be proud. Like the violet, he will hang down his head in humility. A true penitent confesses that he mingles sin with all he does, and therefore has nothing to boast of. Uzziah, though a king, yet had a leprosy in his forehead; he had enough to abase him (*2 Chron. 26.19*). So a child of God, even when he does good, yet acknowledges much evil to be in that good. This lays all his feathers of pride in the dust.

(3) Confession gives vent to a troubled heart. When

guilt lies boiling in the conscience, confession gives ease. It is like the lancing of an abscess which gives ease to the patient.

(4) Confession purges out sin. Augustine called it 'the expeller of vice'. Sin is a bad blood; confession is like the opening of a vein to let it out. Confession is like the dung-gate, through which all the filth of the city was carried forth (*Neh. 3.13*). Confession is like pumping at the leak; it lets out that sin which would otherwise drown. Confession is the sponge that wipes the spots from off the soul.

(5) Confession of sin endears Christ to the soul. If I say I am a sinner, how precious will Christ's blood be to me! After Paul has confessed a body of sin, he breaks forth into a gratulatory triumph for Christ: 'I thank God through Jesus Christ' (*Rom. 7.25*). If a debtor confesses a judgment but the creditor will not exact the debt, instead appointing his own son to pay it, will not the debtor be very thankful? So when we confess the debt, and that even though we should for ever lie in hell we cannot pay it, but that God should appoint his own Son to lay down his blood for the payment of our debt, how is free grace magnified and Jesus Christ eternally loved and admired!

(6) Confession of sin makes way for pardon. No sooner did the prodigal come with a confession in his mouth, 'I have sinned against heaven', than his father's heart did melt towards him, and he kissed him (*Luke 15.20*). When David said, 'I have sinned', the prophet brought him a box with a pardon, 'The Lord hath put away thy sin' (*2 Sam. 12.13*). He who sincerely confesses sin has God's bond for a pardon: 'If we confess our sins, he is faithful and just to forgive us our sins' (*1 John 1.9*). Why does not the apostle say that if we confess he is *merciful* to forgive our sins? No; he is just, because he has bound himself by promise to forgive such. God's truth

and justice are engaged for the pardoning of that man who confesses sin and comes with a penitent heart by faith in Christ.

(7) How reasonable and easy is this command that we should confess sin! (a) It is a *reasonable* command, for if one has wronged another, what is more rational than to confess he has wronged him? We, having wronged God by sin, how equal and consonant to reason is it that we should confess the offence. (b) It is an *easy* command. What a vast difference is there between the first covenant and the second! In the first covenant it was, if you commit sin you die; in the second covenant it is, if you confess sin you shall have mercy. In the first covenant no surety was allowed; under the covenant of grace, if we do but confess the debt, Christ will be our surety. What way could be thought of as more ready and facile for the salvation of man than a humble confession? 'Only acknowledge thine iniquity' (*Jer. 3.13*). God says to us, I do not ask for sacrifices of rams to expiate your guilt; I do not bid you part with the fruit of your body for the sin of your soul, 'only acknowledge thine iniquity'; do but draw up an indictment against yourself and plead guilty, and you shall be sure of mercy.

All this should render this duty amiable. Throw out the poison of sin by confession, and 'this day is salvation come to thy house'.

There remains one case of conscience: are we bound to confess our sins to men? The papists insist much upon auricular confession; one must confess his sins in the ear of the priest or he cannot be absolved. They urge, 'Confess your sins one to another' (*James 5.16*), but this scripture is little to their purpose. It may as well mean that the priest should confess to the people as well as the people to the priest. Auricular confession is one of the

Pope's golden doctrines. Like the fish in the Gospel, it has money in its mouth: 'when thou hast opened his mouth, thou shalt find a piece of money' (*Matt. 17.27*). But though I am not for confession to men in a popish sense, yet I think in three cases there ought to be confession to men:

(1) Firstly, where a person has fallen into scandalous sin and by it has been an occasion of offence to some and of falling to others, he ought to make a solemn and open acknowledgement of his sin, that his repentance may be as visible as his scandal (*2 Cor. 2.6–7*).

(2) Secondly, where a man has confessed his sin to God, yet still his conscience is burdened, and he can have no ease in his mind, it is very requisite that he should confess his sins to some prudent, pious friend, who may advise him and speak a word in due season (*James 5.16*). It is a sinful modesty in Christians that they are not more free with their ministers and other spiritual friends in unburdening themselves and opening the sores and troubles of their souls to them. If there is a thorn sticking in the conscience, it is good to make use of those who may help to pluck it out.

(3) Thirdly, where any man has slandered another and by clipping his good name has made it weigh lighter, he is bound to make confession. The scorpion carries its poison in its tail, the slanderer in his tongue. His words pierce deep like the quills of the porcupine. That person who has murdered another in his good name or, by bearing false witness, has damaged him in his estate, ought to confess his sin and ask forgiveness: 'if thou bring thy gift to the altar, and there rememberest that thy brother hath ought against thee; go thy way; first be reconciled to thy brother, and then come and offer thy gift' (*Matt. 5.23–4*). How can this reconciliation be effected but by confessing the injury? Till this is done,

God will accept none of your services. Do not think the holiness of the altar will privilege you; your praying and hearing are in vain till you have appeased your brother's anger by confessing your fault to him.

Chapter Four

THE NATURE OF TRUE
REPENTANCE (2)

Ingredient 4: Shame for Sin

The fourth ingredient in repentance is shame: 'that they may be ashamed of their iniquities' (*Ezek. 43.10*). Blushing is the colour of virtue. When the heart has been made black with sin, grace makes the face red with blushing: 'I am ashamed and blush to lift up my face' (*Ezra 9.6*). The repenting prodigal was so ashamed of his excess that he thought himself not worthy to be called a son any more (*Luke 15.21*). Repentance causes a holy bashfulness. If Christ's blood were not at the sinner's heart, there would not so much blood come in the face. There are nine considerations about sin which may cause shame:

(1) *Every sin makes us guilty*, and guilt usually breeds shame. Adam never blushed in the time of innocency. While he kept the whiteness of the lily, he had not the blushing of the rose; but when he had defloured his soul by sin, then he was ashamed. Sin has tainted our blood. We are guilty of high treason against the Crown of heaven. This may cause a holy modesty and blushing.

(2) *In every sin there is much unthankfulness*, and that is a matter of shame. He who is upbraided with ingratitude will blush. We have sinned against God when he has given us no cause: 'What iniquity have your fathers found in me?' (*Jer. 2.5*). Wherein has God wearied us, unless his mercies have wearied us? Oh the silver drops

that have fallen on us! We have had the finest of the wheat; we have been fed with angels' food. The golden oil of divine blessing has run down on us from the head of our heavenly Aaron. And to abuse the kindness of so good a God, how may this make us ashamed! Julius Caesar took it unkindly at the hands of Brutus,[1] on whom he had bestowed so many favours, when he came to stab him: 'What, thou, my son Brutus?' O ungrateful, to be the worse for mercy! Aelian[2] reports of the vulture, that it draws sickness from perfumes. To contract the disease of pride and luxury from the perfume of God's mercy, how unworthy is it; to requite evil for good, to kick against our feeder (*Deut. 32.15*); to make an arrow of God's mercies and shoot at him, to wound him with his own blessing! O horrid ingratitude! Will not this dye our faces a deep scarlet? Unthankfulness is a sin so great that God himself stands amazed at it: 'Hear, O heavens, and give ear, O earth: I have nourished and brought up children, and they have rebelled against me' (*Isa. 1.2*).

(3) *Sin has made us naked*, and that may breed shame. Sin has stripped us of our white linen of holiness. It has made us naked and deformed in God's eye, which may cause blushing. When Hanun had abused David's servants and cut off their garments so that their nakedness did appear, the text says, 'the men were greatly ashamed' (*2 Sam. 10.5*).

(4) *Our sins have put Christ to shame*, and should not we be ashamed? The Jews arrayed him in purple; they put a reed in his hand, spat in his face, and in his greatest agonies reviled him. Here was 'the shame of the cross'; and that which aggravated the shame was to consider the eminency of his person, as he was the Lamb of God. Did

---

[1]Brutus, the close friend of Julius Caesar, helped to stab him to death in 44 B.C.

[2]A Roman who wrote about nature (early in the third century).

our sins put Christ to shame, and shall they not put us to shame? Did he wear the purple, and shall not our cheeks wear crimson? Who can behold the sun as it were blushing at Christ's passion, and hiding itself in an eclipse, and his face not blush?

(5) *Many sins which we commit are by the special instigation of the devil,* and should not this cause shame? The devil put it into the heart of Judas to betray Christ (*John 13.2*). He filled Ananias' heart to lie (*Acts 5.3*). He often stirs up our passions (*James 3.6*). Now, as it is a shame to bring forth a child illegitimately, so too is it to bring forth such sins as may call the devil father. It is said that the virgin Mary conceived by the power of the Holy Ghost (*Luke 1.35*), but we often conceive by the power of Satan. When the heart conceives pride, lust, and malice, it is very often by the power of the devil. May not this make us ashamed to think that many of our sins are committed in copulation with the old serpent?

(6) *Sin, like Circe's[1] enchanting cup, turns men into beasts* (*Ps. 49.12*), and is not that matter for shame? Sinners are compared to foxes (*Luke 13.32*), to wolves (*Matt. 7.15*), to asses (*Job 11.12*), to swine (*2 Pet. 2.22*). A sinner is a swine with a man's head. He who was once little less than the angels in dignity is now become like the beasts. Grace in this life does not wholly obliterate this brutish temper. Agur, that good man, cried out, 'Surely I am more brutish than any!' (*Prov. 30.2*). But common sinners are in a manner wholly brutified; they do not act rationally but are carried away by the violence of their lusts and passions. How may this make us ashamed who are thus degenerated below our own species? Our sins have taken away that noble, masculine spirit which once we had. The crown is fallen from our head. God's image

[1] An enchantress in Greek legend who gave her magic cup to Ulysses' companions and changed them into swine.

is defaced, reason is eclipsed, conscience stupified. We have more in us of the brute than of the angel.

(7) *In every sin there is folly* (*Jer.* 4.22). A man will be ashamed of his folly. Is not he a fool who labours more for the bread that perishes than for the bread of life? Is not he a fool who for a lust or a trifle will lose heaven, like Tiberius[1] who for a draught of drink forfeited his kingdom? Is not he a fool who, to safeguard his body, will injure his soul? As if one should let his arm or head be cut to save his vest! *Naviget antyciram*[2] (Horace). Is not he a fool who will believe a temptation before a promise? Is not he a fool who minds his recreation more than his salvation? How may this make men ashamed, to think that they inherit not land, but folly (*Prov.* 14.18).

(8) That which may make us blush is that *the sins we commit are far worse than the sins of the heathen*. We act against more light. To us have been committed the oracles of God. The sin committed by a Christian is worse than the same sin committed by an Indian because the Christian sins against clearer conviction, which is like the dye to the wool or the weight put into the scale that makes it weigh heavier.

(9) *Our sins are worse than the sins of the devils*: the lapsed angels never sinned against Christ's blood. Christ died not for them. The medicine of his merit was never intended to heal them. But we have affronted and disparaged his blood by unbelief.

The devils never sinned against God's patience. As soon as they apostatised, they were damned. God never

---

[1]The third Roman emperor, mentioned in Luke 3.1. He reigned from A.D. 14 to 37. For much of his reign he was accused of chronic intoxication.

[2]'Let him sail to Anticyra.' Hellebore, a plant found at Anticyra, a town on the Gulf of Corinth, was believed to be a cure for insanity.

waited for the angels, but we have spent upon the stock of God's patience. He has pitied our weakness, borne with our forwardness. His Spirit has been repulsed, yet has still importuned us and will take no denial. Our conduct has been so provoking as to have tired not only the patience of a Moses but of all the angels. We have put God to it, and made him weary of repenting (*Jer.* 15.6).

The devils never sinned against example. They were the first that sinned and were made the first example. We have seen the angels, those morning stars, fall from their glorious orb; we have seen the old world drowned, Sodom burned, yet have ventured upon sin. How desperate is that thief who robs in the very place where his fellow hangs in chains. And surely, if we have outsinned the devils, it may well put us to the blush.

Use 1. Is shame an ingredient of repentance? If so, how far are they from being penitents who have no shame? Many have sinned away shame: 'the unjust knoweth no shame' (*Zeph.* 3.5). It is a great shame not to be ashamed. The Lord sets it as a brand upon the Jews: 'Were they ashamed when they had committed abomination? Nay, they were not at all ashamed, neither could they blush' (*Jer.* 6.15). The devil has stolen shame from men. When one of the persecutors in Queen Mary's time was upbraided with his bloodiness to the martyrs, he replied, 'I see nothing to be ashamed of'. Many are no more ashamed of their sin than King Nebuchadnezzar was of his being turned to grass. When men have hearts of stone and foreheads of brass, it is a sign that the devil has taken full possession of them. There is no creature capable of shame but man. The brute beasts are capable of fear and pain, but not of shame. You cannot make a beast blush. Those who cannot blush for sin do too much resemble the beasts.

[43]

There are some so far from this holy blushing that they are proud of their sins. They are proud of their long hair. These are the devil's Nazarites. 'Doth not even nature itself teach you, that, if a man have long hair, it is a shame unto him' (*1 Cor. 11.14*). It confounds the distinction of the sexes. Others are proud of their black spots. And what if God should turn them into blue spots?

Others are so far from being ashamed of sin that they glory in their sins: 'whose glory is in their shame' (*Phil. 3.19*). Some are ashamed of that which is their glory: they are ashamed to be seen with a good book in their hand. Others glory in that which is their shame: they look on sin as a piece of gallantry. The swearer thinks his speech most graceful when it is interlarded with oaths. The drunkard counts it a glory that he is mighty to drink (*Isa. 5.22*). But when men shall be cast into a fiery furnace, heated seven times hotter by the breath of the Almighty, then let them boast of sin as they see cause.

Use 2. Let us show our penitence by a modest blushing: 'O my God, I blush to lift up my face' (*Ezra 9.6*). 'My God' – there was faith; 'I blush' – there was repentance. Hypocrites will confidently avouch God to be their God, but they know not how to blush. O let us take holy shame to ourselves for sin. Be assured, the more we are ashamed of sin now, the less we shall be ashamed at Christ's coming. If the sins of the godly be mentioned at the day of judgment, it will not be to shame them, but to magnify the riches of God's grace in pardoning them. Indeed, the wicked shall be ashamed at the last day. They shall sneak and hang down their heads, but the saints shall then be as without spot (*Eph. 5.27*), so without shame; therefore they are bid to lift up their heads (*Luke 21.28*).

Ingredient 5: Hatred of Sin

The fifth ingredient in repentance is hatred of sin. The Schoolmen[1] distinguished a two-fold hatred: hatred of abominations, and hatred of enmity.

Firstly, there is a hatred or loathing of abominations: 'Ye shall loathe yourselves for your iniquities' (*Ezek.* 36.31). A true penitent is a sin-loather. If a man loathe that which makes his stomach sick, much more will he loathe that which makes his conscience sick. It is more to loathe sin than to leave it. One may leave sin for fear, as in a storm the plate and jewels are cast overboard, but the nauseating and loathing of sin argues a detestation of it. Christ is never loved till sin be loathed. Heaven is never longed for till sin be loathed. When the soul sees an issue of blood running, he cries out, Lord, when shall I be freed from this body of death? When shall I put off these filthy garments of sin and have the fair mitre of glory set upon my head? Let all my self-love be turned into self-loathing (*Zech.* 3.4–5). We are never more precious in God's eyes than when we are lepers in our own.

Secondly, there is a hatred of enmity. There is no better way to discover life than by motion. The eye moves, the pulse beats. So to discover repentance there is no better sign than by a holy antipathy against sin. Hatred, said Cicero,[2] is anger boiled up to an inveteracy. Sound repentance begins in the love of God and ends in the hatred of sin.

How may true hatred of sin be known?

1. *When a man's spirit is set against sin*

The tongue does not only inveigh against sin, but the heart abhors it, so that however curiously painted sin appears, we find it odious, as we abhor the picture of one whom we mortally hate, even though it may be well

[1] Theologians of the Middle Ages.
[2] A famous orator and statesman of the last century before Christ.

THE DOCTRINE OF REPENTANCE

drawn. 'I love not thee, Sabidi.'[1] Suppose a dish be finely cooked and the sauce good, yet if a man has an antipathy against the meat, he will not taste it. So let the devil cook and dress sin with pleasure and profit, yet a true penitent with a secret abhorrence of it is disgusted by it and will not meddle with it.

2. *True hatred of sin is universal*

True hatred of sin is universal in two ways: in respect of the faculties, and of the object.

(1) Hatred is universal in respect of the faculties, that is, there is a dislike of sin not only in the judgment, but in the will and affections. Many a one is convinced that sin is a vile thing, and in his judgment has an aversion to it, but yet he tastes sweetness and has a secret complacency in it. Here is a disliking of sin in the judgment and an embracing of it in the affections; whereas in true repentance the hatred of sin is in all the faculties, not only in the intellectual part, but chiefly in the will: 'what I hate, that do I' (*Rom. 7.15*). Paul was not free from sin, yet his will was against it.

(2) Hatred is universal in respect of the object. He who hates one sin hates all. Aristotle[2] said, hatred is against the whole kind. He who hates a serpent hates all serpents: 'I hate every false way' (*Ps. 119.104*). Hypocrites will hate some sins which mar their credit, but a true convert hates all sins, gainful sins, complexion-sins, the very stirrings of corruption. Paul hated the motions of sin (*Rom. 7.23*).

3. *True hatred against sin is against sin in all forms*

[1] An epigram of the Roman writer Martial. Its English counterpart is found in the lines:

> I do not love you, Dr Fell,
> But why it is I cannot tell;
> But this I know, and know full well,
> I do not love you, Dr Fell.

[2] A Greek of the fourth century B.C., famous as philosopher, logician, metaphysician and 'the father of natural science'.

A holy heart detests sin for its intrinsic pollution. Sin leaves a stain upon the soul. A regenerate person abhors sin not only for the curse but for the contagion. He hates this serpent not only for its sting but for its poison. He hates sin not only *for* hell, but *as* hell.

4. *True hatred is implacable*

It will never be reconciled to sin any more. Anger may be reconciled, but hatred cannot. Sin is that Amalek which is never to be taken into favour again. The war between a child of God and sin is like the war between those two princes: 'there was war between Rehoboam and Jeroboam all their days' (*1 Kings 14.30*).

5. *Where there is a real hatred, we not only oppose sin in ourselves but in others too*

The church at Ephesus could not bear with those who were evil (*Rev. 2.2*). Paul sharply censured Peter for his dissimulation although he was an apostle. Christ in a holy displeasure whipped the money-changers out of the temple (*John 2.15*). He would not suffer the temple to be made an exchange. Nehemiah rebuked the nobles for their usury (*Neh. 5.7*) and their Sabbath profanation (*Neh. 13.17*). A sin-hater will not endure wickedness in his family: 'He that worketh deceit shall not dwell within my house' (*Ps. 101.7*). What a shame it is when magistrates can show height of spirit in their passions but no heroic spirit in suppressing vice. Those who have no antipathy against sin are strangers to repentance. Sin is in them as poison in a serpent, which, being natural to it, affords delight.

How far are they from repentance who, instead of hating sin, love sin! To the godly sin is as a thorn in the eye; to the wicked it is as a crown on the head: 'When thou doest evil, then thou rejoicest' (*Jer. 11.15*). Loving of sin is worse than committing it. A good man may run

[47]

into a sinful action unawares, but to love sin is desperate. What is it that makes a swine but loving to tumble in the mire? What is it that makes a devil but loving that which opposes God? To love sin shows that the will is in sin, and the more of the will there is in a sin, the greater the sin. Wilfulness makes it a sin not to be purged by sacrifice (*Heb. 10.26*).

O how many there are that love the forbidden fruit! They love their oaths and adulteries; they love the sin and hate the reproof. Solomon speaks of a generation of men: 'madness is in their heart while they live' (*Eccles. 9.3*). So for men to love sin, to hug that which will be their death, to sport with damnation, 'madness is in their heart'.

It persuades us to show our repentance by a bitter hatred of sin. There is a deadly antipathy between the scorpion and the crocodile; such should there be between the heart and sin.

Question: What is there in sin that may make a penitent hate it?

Answer: Sin is the cursed thing, the most misshapen monster. The apostle Paul uses a very emphatic word to express it: 'that sin might become exceeding sinful' (*Rom. 7.13*), or as it is in the Greek, 'hyperbolically sinful'. That sin is a hyperbolical mischief and deserves hatred will appear if we look upon sin as a fourfold conceit:

(1) Look upon the origin of sin, from whence it comes. It fetches its pedigree from hell: 'He that committeth sin is of the devil, for the devil sinneth from the beginning' (*1 John 3.8*). Sin is the devil's proper work. God has a hand in ordering sin, it is true, but Satan has a hand in acting it out. How hateful is it to be doing that which is the peculiar work of the devil, indeed, that which makes men devils?

(2) Look upon sin in its nature, and it will appear very hateful. See how scripture has pencilled it out: it is a dishonouring of God (*Rom. 2.23*); a despising of God (*1*

Sam. 2.30); a fretting of God (*Ezek. 16.43*); a wearying of God (*Isa. 7.13*); a breaking the heart of God, as a loving husband is with the unchaste conduct of his wife: 'I am broken with their whorish heart' (*Ezek. 6.9*). Sin, when acted to the height, is a crucifying Christ afresh and putting him to open shame (*Heb. 6.6*), that is, impudent sinners pierce Christ in his saints, and were he now upon earth they would crucify him again in his person. Behold the odious nature of sin.

(3) Look upon sin in its comparison, and it appears ghastly. Compare sin with affliction and hell, and it is worse than both. It is worse than affliction: sickness, poverty, death. There is more malignity in a drop of sin than in a sea of affliction, for sin is the cause of affliction, and the cause is more than the effect. The sword of God's justice lies quiet in the scabbard till sin draws it out. Affliction is good for us: 'It is good for me that I have been afflicted' (*Ps. 119.71*). Affliction causes repentance (*2 Chron. 33.12*). The viper, being stricken, casts up its poison; so, God's rod striking us, we spit away the poison of sin. Affliction betters our grace. Gold is purest, and juniper sweetest, in the fire. Affliction prevents damnation (*1 Cor. 11.32*). Therefore, Maurice the emperor[1] prayed to God to punish him in this life that he might not be punished hereafter. Thus, affliction is in many ways for our good, but there is no good in sin. Manasseh's affliction brought him to humiliation, but Judas' sin brought him to desperation.

Affliction only reaches the body, but sin goes further: it poisons the fancy, disorders the affections. Affliction is but corrective; sin is destructive. Affliction can but take away the life; sin takes away the soul (*Luke 12.20*). A man that is afflicted may have his conscience quiet. When

---

[1] Roman emperor in the sixth century.

the ark was tossed on the waves, Noah could sing in the ark. When the body is afflicted and tossed, a Christian can 'make melody in his heart to the Lord' (*Eph. 5.19*). But when a man commits sin, conscience is terrified. Witness Spira,[1] who upon his abjuring the faith said that he thought the damned spirits did not feel those torments which he inwardly endured.

In affliction one may have the love of God (*Rev. 3.19*). If a man should throw a bag of money at another, and in throwing it should hurt him a little and raise the skin, he will not take it unkindly, but will look upon it as a fruit of love. So when God bruises us with affliction, it is to enrich us with the golden graces and comforts of his Spirit. All is in love. But when we commit sin, God withdraws his love. When David sinned he felt nothing but displeasure from God: 'Clouds and darkness are round about him' (*Ps. 97.2*). David found it so. He could see no rainbow, no sunbeam, nothing but clouds and darkness about God's face.

That sin is worse than affliction is evident because the greatest judgment God lays upon a man in this life is to let him sin without control. When the Lord's displeasure is most severely kindled against a person, he does not say, I will bring the sword and the plague on this man, but, I will let him sin on: 'So I gave them up unto their own hearts' lust' (*Ps. 81.12*). Now, if the giving up of a man to his sins (in the account of God himself) is the most dreadful evil, then sin is far worse than affliction. And if it be so, then how should it be hated by us!

[1]An eminent lawyer living near Venice in the Reformation period (sixteenth century). He turned from Romanism, accepted the Protestant faith, but later apostatized and died in despair in 1548. His *Life* was published in Geneva in 1550, John Calvin supplying a preface. John Bunyan was deeply impressed by what happened to Spira. The man in the iron cage in the Interpreter's House in *Pilgrim's Progress* undoubtedly represents him.

Compare sin with hell, and you shall see that sin is worse. Torment has its emphasis in hell, yet nothing there is as bad as sin. Hell is of God's making, but sin is none of his making. Sin is the devil's creature. The torments of hell are a burden only to the sinner, but sin is a burden to God: 'I am pressed under you, as a cart is pressed that is full of sheaves' (*Amos. 2.13*). In the torments of hell there is something that is good, namely, the execution of divine justice. There is justice to be found in hell, but sin is a piece of the highest injustice. It would rob God of his glory, Christ of his purchase, the soul of its happiness. Judge then if sin be not a most hateful thing, which is worse than affliction or hell.

(4) Look upon sin in the issue and consequence, and it will appear hateful. Sin reaches the body. It has exposed it to a variety of miseries. We come into the world with a cry and go out with a groan. It made the Thracians weep on their children's birthday, as Herodotus tells us, to consider the calamities they were to undergo in the world. Sin is the Trojan horse[1] out of which comes a whole army of troubles. I need not name them because almost everyone feels them. While we suck the honey we are pricked with the briar. Sin gives a dash in the wine of our comforts; it digs our grave (*Rom. 5.12*).

Sin reaches the soul. By sin we have lost the image of God, wherein did consist both our sanctity and our majesty. Adam in his pristine glory was like a herald who has his coat of arms upon him. All reverence him because he carries the king's coat of arms, but pull this coat off, and no man regards him. Sin has done this disgrace to us. It has plucked off our coat of innocency. But that is not

[1]The Greek poet Homer's story of the wooden horse filled with soldiers by means of which the Greeks captured Troy in the province of Ilium (near the Dardanelles) is one of the most famous stories handed down from the ancient world.

all. This bearded arrow of sin would strike yet deeper. It would for ever separate us from the beautiful vision of God, in whose presence is fulness of joy. If sin be so hyperbolically sinful, it should swell our spleen and stir up our implacable indignation against it. As Ammon's hatred of Tamar was greater than the love wherewith he had loved her (*2 Sam. 13.15*), so we should hate sin infinitely more than ever we loved it.

Ingredient 6: Turning from Sin

The sixth ingredient in repentance is a turning from sin. Reformation is left last to bring up the rear of repentance. What though one could, with Niobe,[1] weep himself into a stone, if he did not weep out sin? True repentance, like *aqua fortis* [nitric acid], eats asunder the iron chain of sin. Therefore weeping and turning are put together (*Joel 2.12*). After the cloud of sorrow has dropped in tears, the firmament of the soul is clearer: 'Repent, and turn yourselves from your idols; and turn away your faces from all your abominations' (*Ezek. 14.6*). This turning from sin is called a forsaking of sin (*Isa. 55.7*), as a man forsakes the company of a thief or sorcerer. It is called 'a putting of sin far away' (*Job 11.14*), as Paul put away the viper and shook it into the fire (*Acts 28.5*). Dying to sin is the life of repentance. The very day a Christian turns from sin he must enjoin himself a perpetual fast. The eye must fast from impure glances. The ear must fast from hearing slanders. The tongue must fast from oaths. The hands must fast from bribes. The feet must fast from the path of the harlot. And the soul must fast from the love of wickedness. This turning from sin implies a notable change.

[1] The wife of a king of Thebes in ancient times, who boasted of her twelve children, whereupon, according to Greek legend, she lost them all suddenly, and her grief changed her into a stone which shed tears in summer.

There is a change wrought in the heart. The flinty heart has become fleshly. Satan would have Christ prove his deity by turning stones into bread. Christ has wrought a far greater miracle in making stones become flesh. In repentance Christ turns a heart of stone into flesh.

There is a change wrought in the life. Turning from sin is so visible that others may discern it. Therefore it is called a change from darkness to light (*Eph. 5.8*). Paul, after he had seen the heavenly vision, was so turned that all men wondered at the change (*Acts 9.21*). Repentance turned the jailer into a nurse and physician (*Acts 16.33*). He took the apostles and washed their wounds and set meat before them. A ship is going eastward; there comes a wind which turns it westward. Likewise, a man was turning hell-ward before the contrary wind of the Spirit blew, turned his course, and caused him to sail heavenward. Chrysostom, speaking of the Ninevites' repentance, said that if a stranger who had seen Nineveh's excess had gone into the city after they repented, he would scarce have believed it was the same city because it was so metamorphosed and reformed. Such a visible change does repentance make in a person, as if another soul did lodge in the same body.

That the turning from sin be rightly qualified, these few things are requisite:

1. It must be a turning from sin with the heart

The heart is the *primum vivens*, the first thing that lives, and it must be the *primum vertens*, the first thing that turns. The heart is that which the devil strives hardest for. Never did he so strive for the body of Moses as he does for the heart of man. In religion the heart is all. If the heart be not turned from sin, it is no better than a lie: 'her treacherous sister Judah hath not turned unto me with her whole heart, but feignedly' (*Jer. 3.10*), or as in the Hebrew, 'in a lie'. Judah did make a show of reformation; she was not so grossly idolatrous as the ten tribes. Yet Judah was worse than Israel: she is called 'treacherous' Judah. She pretended to a reformation, but it was not in truth. Her heart was not for God: she turned not with the whole heart.

It is odious to make a show of turning from sin while the heart is yet in league with it. I have read of one of our Saxon kings who was baptized, who in the same church had one altar for the Christian religion and another for the heathen. God will have the whole heart turned from sin. True repentance must have no reserves or inmates.

2. It must be a turning from all sin

'Let the wicked forsake his way' (Isa. 55.7). A real penitent turns out of the road of sin. Every sin is abandoned: as Jehu would have all the priests of Baal slain (2 Kings 10.24) – not one must escape – so a true convert seeks the destruction of every lust. He knows how dangerous it is to entertain any one sin. He that hides one rebel in his house is a traitor to the Crown, and he that indulges one sin is a traitorous hypocrite.

3. It must be a turning from sin upon a spiritual ground

A man may restrain the acts of sin, yet not turn from sin in a right manner. Acts of sin may be restrained out of fear or design, but a true penitent turns from sin out of a religious principle, namely, love to God. Even if sin did not bear such bitter fruit, if death did not grow on this tree, a gracious soul would forsake it out of love to God. This is the most kindly turning from sin. When things are frozen and congealed, the best way to separate them is by fire. When men and their sins are congealed together, the best way to separate them is by the fire of love. Three men, asking one another what made them leave sin: one says, I think of the joys of heaven; another, I think of the torments of hell; but the third, I think of the love of God, and that makes me forsake it. How shall I offend the God of love?

4. *It must be such a turning from sin as turns unto God*
This is in the text, 'that they should repent and turn to God' (*Acts 26.20*). Turning from sin is like pulling the arrow out of the wound; turning to God is like pouring in the balm. We read in scripture of a repentance from dead works (*Heb. 6.1*), and a repentance toward God (*Acts 20.21*). Unsound hearts pretend to leave old sins, but they do not turn to God or embrace his service. It is not enough to forsake the devil's quarters, but we must get under Christ's banner and wear his colours. The repenting prodigal did not only leave his harlots, but he arose and went to his father. It was God's complaint, 'They return, but not to the most High' (*Hos. 7.16*). In true repentance the heart points directly to God as the needle to the North Pole.

5. *True turning from sin is such a turn as has no return*
'Ephraim shall say, What have I to do any more with idols?' (*Hos. 14.8*). Forsaking sin must be like forsaking one's native soil, never more to return to it. Some have seemed to be converts and to have turned from sin, but they have returned to their sins again. This is a returning to folly (*Ps. 85.8*). It is a fearful sin, for it is against clear light. It is to be supposed that he who did once leave his sin felt it bitter in the pangs of conscience. Yet he returned to it again; he therefore sins against the illuminations of the Spirit.

Such a return to sin reproaches God: 'What iniquity have your fathers found in me, that they are gone far from me?' (*Jer. 2.5*). He that returns to sin by implication charges God with some evil. If a man puts away his wife, it implies he knows some fault by her. To leave God and return to sin is tacitly to asperse the Deity. God, who 'hateth putting away' (*Mal. 2.16*), hates that he himself should be put away.

To return to sin gives the devil more power over a man that ever. When a man turns from sin, the devil seems to be cast out of him, but when he returns to sin, the devil enters into his house again and takes possession, and 'the last state of that man is worse than the first' (*Matt. 12.45*). When a prisoner has broken prison, and the jailer gets him again, he will lay stronger irons upon him. He who leaves off a course of sinning, as it were, breaks the devil's prison, but if Satan takes him returning to sin, he will hold him faster and take fuller possession of him than ever. Oh take heed of this! A true turning from sin is a divorcing it, so as never to come near it any more. Whoever is thus turned from sin is a blessed person: 'God, having raised up his Son Jesus, sent him to bless you, in turning away every one of you from his iniquities' (*Acts 3.26*).

Use 1. Is turning from sin a necessary ingredient in repentance? If so, then there is little repentance to be found. People are not turned from their sins; they are still the same as they were. They were proud, and so they are still. Like the beasts in Noah's ark, they went into the ark unclean and came out unclean. Men come to ordinances impure and go away impure. Though men have seen so many changes without, yet there is no change wrought within: 'the people turneth not unto him that smiteth' (*Isa. 9.13*). How can they say they repent who do not turn? Are they washed in Jordan who still have their leprosy upon their forehead? May not God say to the unreformed, as once to Ephraim, 'Ephraim is joined to idols: let him alone' (*Hos. 4.17*)? Likewise, here is a man joined to his drunkenness and uncleanness, let him alone; let him go on in sin; but if there be either justice in heaven or vengeance in hell, he shall not go unpunished.

Use 2. It reproves those who are but half-turned. And who are these? Such as turn in their judgment but not in their practice. They cannot but acknowledge that sin, like

Saturn,[1] has a bad aspect and influence and will weep for
sin, yet they are so bewitched with it that they have no
power to leave it. Their corruptions are stronger than
their convictions. These are half-turned, 'almost Christians' (*Acts 26.28*). They are like Ephraim, who was a
cake baked on one side and dough on the other (*Hos.
7.8*).

They are but half-turned who turn only from gross sin
but have no intrinsic work of grace. They do not prize
Christ or love holiness. It is with civil persons as with
Jonah; he got a gourd to defend him from the heat of the
sun, and thought that he was safe, but a worm presently
arose and devoured the gourd. So men, when they are
turned from gross sin, think their civility will be a gourd
to defend them from the wrath of God, but at death there
arises the worm of conscience, which smites this gourd,
and then their hearts fail, and they begin to despair.

They are but half-turned who turn from many sins but
are unturned from some special sin. There is a harlot in
the bosom they will not let go. As if a man should be
cured of several diseases but has a cancer in his breast,
which kills him. It reproves those whose turning is as
good as no turning, who expel one devil and welcome
another. They turn from swearing to slandering, from
profuseness to covetousness, like a sick man that turns
from a tertian ague[2] to a quartan. Such turning will turn
men to hell.

Use 3. Let us show ourselves penitents in turning from
sin to God. There are some persons I have little hope to
prevail with. Let the trumpet of the word sound never so

[1] Non-Christian astrologers have long supposed that the planets exert an
influence, good or ill, on human life. The planet Saturn has been supposed
to exert a baleful influence on men; hence the adjective 'saturnine'.
[2] A burning fever occurring every third (by inclusive reckoning, fourth)
day.

shrill, let threatenings be thundered out against them, let some flashes of hell-fire be thrown in their faces, yet they will have the other game at sin. These persons seem to be like the swine in the Gospel, carried down by the devil violently into the sea. They will rather damn than turn: 'they hold fast deceit, they refuse to return' (*Jer. 8.5*). But if there be any candour or sobriety in us, if conscience be not cast into a deep sleep, let us listen to the voice of the charmer, and turn to God our supreme good.

How often does God call upon us to turn to him? He swears, 'As I live, I have no pleasure in the death of the wicked: turn ye, turn ye from your evil ways' (*Ezek. 33.11*). God would rather have our repenting tears than our blood.

Turning to God makes for our profit. Our repentance is of no benefit to God, but to ourselves. If a man drinks of a fountain he benefits himself, not the fountain. If he beholds the light of the sun, he himself is refreshed by it, not the sun. If we turn from our sins to God, God is not advantaged by it. It is only we ourselves who reap the benefit. In this case self-love should prevail with us: 'If thou be wise, thou shalt be wise for thyself' (*Prov. 9.12*).

If we turn to God, he will turn to us. He will turn his anger from us, and his face to us. It was David's prayer, 'O turn unto me, and have mercy upon me' (*Ps. 86.16*). Our turning will make God turn: 'Turn ye unto me, saith the Lord, and I will turn unto you' (*Zech. 1.3*). He who was an enemy will turn to be our friend. If God turns to us, the angels are turned to us. We shall have their tutelage and guardianship (*Ps. 91.11*). If God turns to us, all things shall turn to our good, both mercies and afflictions; we shall taste honey at the end of the rod.

Thus we have seen the several ingredients of repentance.

Chapter Five

THE REASONS ENFORCING REPENTANCE, WITH A WARNING TO THE IMPENITENT

I proceed next to the reasons which enforce repentance.

1. *God's sovereign command*

'He commandeth all men every where to repent' (*Acts 17.30*). Repentance is not arbitrary. It is not left to our choice whether or not we will repent, but it is an indispensable command. God has enacted a law in the High Court of heaven that no sinner shall be saved except the repenting sinner, and he will not break his own law. Though all the angels should stand before God and beg the life of an unrepenting person, God would not grant it. 'The Lord God, merciful and gracious, keeping mercy for thousands, and that will by no means clear the guilty' (*Exod. 34.6–7*). Though God is more full of mercy than the sun is of light, yet he will not forgive a sinner while he goes on in his guilt: 'He will by no means clear the guilty'!

2. *The pure nature of God denies communion with an impenitent creature*

Till the sinner repents, God and he cannot be friends: 'Wash you, make you clean' (*Isa. 1.16*); go, steep yourselves in the brinish waters of repentance. Then, says God, I will parley with you: 'Come now, and let us reason together' (*Isa. 1.18*); but otherwise, come not near me: 'What communion hath light with darkness?' (*2 Cor. 6.14*). How can the righteous God indulge him that goes on still in his trespasses? 'I will not justify the wicked'

(*Exod.* 23.7). If God should be at peace with a sinner before he repents, God would seem to like and approve all that he has done. He would go against his own holiness. It is inconsistent with the sanctity of God's nature to pardon a sinner while he is in the act of rebellion.

3. *Sinners continuing in impenitence are out of Christ's commission*

See his commission: 'The Spirit of the Lord God is upon me; he hath sent me to bind up the brokenhearted' (*Isa.* 61.1). Christ is a Prince and Saviour, but not to save men in an absolute way, whether or not they repent. If ever Christ brings men to heaven, it shall be through the gates of hell: 'Him hath God exalted to be a Prince and a Saviour to give repentance' (*Acts* 5.31); as a king pardons rebels if they repent and yield themselves to the mercy of their prince, but not if they persist in open defiance.

4. *We have by sin wronged God*

There is a great deal of equity in it that we should repent. We have by sin wronged God. We have eclipsed his honour. We have infringed his law, and we should, reasonably, make him some reparation. By repentance we humble and judge ourselves for sin. We set to our seal that God is righteous if he should destroy us, and thus we give glory to God and do what lies in us to repair his honour.

5. *If God should save men without repentance, making no discrimination, then by this rule he must save all,*

not only men, but devils, as Origen once held; and so consequently the decrees of election and reprobation must fall to the ground. How diametrically opposed this is to sacred writ, let all judge.

There are two sorts of persons who will find it harder to repent than others:

(1) Those who have sat a great while under the ministry of God's ordinances but grow no better. The earth which drinks in the rain, yet 'beareth thorns and briars, is nigh unto cursing' (*Heb. 6.8*). There is little hope of the metal which has lain long in the fire but is not melted and refined. When God has sent his ministers one after another, exhorting and persuading men to leave their sins, but they settle upon the lees¹ of formality and can sit and sleep under a sermon, it will be hard for these ever to be brought to repentance. They may fear lest Christ should say to them as once he said to the fig-tree, 'Never fruit grow on thee more' (*Matt. 21.19*).

(2) Those who have sinned frequently against the convictions of the word, the checks of conscience, and the motions of the Spirit. Conscience has stood as the angel with a flaming sword in its hand. It has said, Do not this great evil, but sinners regard not the voice of conscience, but march on resolvedly under the devil's colours. These will not find it easy to repent: 'They are of those that rebel against the light' (*Job 24.13*). It is one thing to sin for want of light and another thing to sin against light. Here the unpardonable sin takes its rise. Men begin by sinning against the light of conscience, and proceed gradually to despising² the Spirit of grace.

A Reprehension to the Impenitent

Firstly, it serves sharply to reprove all unrepenting sinners whose hearts seem to be hewn out of a rock and are like the stony ground in the parable which lacked moisture. This disease, I fear, is epidemical: 'No man repented him of his wickedness' (*Jer. 8.6*). Men's hearts are marbled into hardness: 'they made their hearts as an

¹Dregs.
²Showing contempt or scorn for; also, provoking to anger.

adamant stone' (*Zech. 7.12*). They are not at all dissolved into a penitential frame. It is a received opinion that witches never weep. I am sure that those who have no grief for sin are spiritually bewitched by Satan. We read that when Christ came to Jerusalem he 'upbraided the cities because they repented not' (*Matt. 11.20*). And may he not upbraid many now for their impenitence? Though God's heart be broken with their sins, yet their hearts are not broken. They say, as Israel did, 'I have loved strangers, and after them will I go' (*Jer. 2.25*). The justice of God, like the angel, stands with a drawn sword in its hand, ready to strike, but sinners have not eyes as good as those of Balaam's ass to see the sword. God smites on men's backs, but they do not, as Ephraim did, smite upon their thigh (*Jer. 31.19*). It was a sad complaint the prophet took up: 'thou hast stricken them, but they have not grieved' (*Jer. 5.3*). That is surely reprobate silver which contracts hardness in the furnace. 'In the time of his distress did he trespass yet more against the Lord: this is that king Ahaz' (*2 Chron. 28.22*). A hard heart is a receptacle for Satan. As God has two places he dwells in, heaven and a humble heart, so the devil has two places he dwells in, hell and a hard heart. It is not falling into water that drowns, but lying in it. It is not falling into sin that damns, but lying in it without repentance: 'having their conscience seared with a hot iron' (*1 Tim. 4.2*). Hardness of heart results at last in the conscience being seared. Men have silenced their consciences, and God has seared them. And now he lets them sin and does not punish – 'Why should ye be stricken any more?' (*Isa. 1.5*) – as a father gives over correcting a child whom he intends to disinherit.

Chapter Six

A SERIOUS EXHORTATION
TO REPENTANCE

Let me in the next place persuade you to this great duty of repentance. Sorrow is good for nothing but sin. If you shed tears for outward losses, it will not advantage you. Water for the garden, if poured in the sink, does no good. Powder for the eye, if applied to the arm, is of no benefit. Sorrow is medicinable for the soul, but if you apply it to worldly things it does no good. Oh that our tears may run in the right channel and our hearts burst with sorrow for sin!

That I may the more successfully press this exhortation, I shall show you that repentance is necessary, and that it is necessary for all persons and for all sins.

1. *Repentance is necessary*
Repentance is necessary: 'except ye repent, ye shall all likewise perish' (*Luke 13.5*). There is no rowing to paradise except upon the stream of repenting tears. Repentance is required as a qualification. It is not so much to endear us to Christ as to endear Christ to us. Till sin be bitter, Christ will not be sweet.

2. *Repentance is necessary for all persons*
Thus God commands all men: 'now God commandeth all men every where to repent' (*Acts 17.30*).

(1) It is necessary for great ones: 'Say unto the king and to the queen, Humble yourselves' (*Jer. 13.18*). The king of Nineveh and his nobles changed their robes for sackcloth (*Jon. 3.6*). Great men's sins do more hurt than

the sins of others. The sins of leaders are leading sins, therefore they of all others have need to repent. If such as hold the sceptre repent not, God has appointed a day to judge them and a fire to burn them (*Isa. 30.33*).

(2) Repentance is necessary for the flagitious sinners in the nation. England needs to put itself in mourning and be humbled by solemn repentance. *Anglica gens est optima flens.*[1] What horrible impieties are chargeable upon the nation! We see persons daily listing themselves under Satan. Not only the banks of religion but those of civility are broken down. Men seem to contend, as the Jews of old, who should be most wicked: 'In their filthiness is lewdness' (*Ezek. 24.13*). If oaths and drunkenness, if perjury and luxury will make a people guilty, then it is to be feared England is in God's black book. Men have cancelled their vow in baptism and made a private contract with the devil! Instead of crying to mercy to save them, they cry, 'God damn them!' Never was there such riding post to hell, as if men did despair of getting there in time. Has it not been known that some have died with the guilt of fornication and blood upon them? Has it not been told that others have boasted how many they have debauched and made drunk? Thus 'they declare their sin as Sodom' (*Isa. 3.9*). Indeed, men's sins are grown daring, as if they would hang out their flag of defiance and give heaven a broadside, like the Thracians who, when it thunders, gather together in a body and shoot their arrows against heaven. The sinners in Britain even send God a challenge: 'They strengthen themselves against the Almighty; they run upon him even on his neck, upon the thick bosses of his bucklers' (*Job 15.25–6*). The bosses in the buckler are for offence in war. God's precepts and threatenings are, as it were, the thick bosses

---

[1]'The English people are best at weeping.'

of his buckler whereby he would deter men from wickedness. They regard not, however, but are desperate in sin and run furiously against the bosses of God's buckler. Oh to what a height is sin boiled up! Men count it a shame not to be impudent. May it not be said of us as Josephus[1] speaks of the Jews. Such was the excessive wickedness of those times that if the Romans had not come and sacked their city, Jerusalem would have been swallowed up with some earthquake, or drowned with a flood, or fired from heaven. And is it not high time then for this nation to enter into a course of physic and take this pill of repentance, who has so many bad humours spreading in her body politic? England is an island encompassed by two oceans, an ocean of water, and an ocean of wickedness. O that it might be encompassed with a third ocean, that of repenting tears!

If the book of the law chance to fall upon the ground, the Jews have a custom presently to proclaim a fast. England has let both law and gospel fall to the ground, therefore needs to fast and mourn before the Lord. The ephah of wickedness seems to be full. There is good reason for tears to empty apace when sin fills so fast! Why then do not all faces gather paleness? Why are the wells of repentance stopped? Do not the sinners of the land know that they should repent? Have they no warning? Have not God's faithful messengers lifted up their voice as a trumpet and cried to them to repent? But many of these tools in the ministry have been spent and worn out upon rocky hearts. Has not God lighted strange comets in the heavens as so many preachers to call men to repentance, but still they are settled on their lees (*Zeph. 1.12*)? Do we think that God will always put up with our affronts? Will

[1] A Jewish historian, author of *The Jewish War*. He lived from A.D.37 to 100.

he endure thus to have his name and glory trampled upon? The Lord has usually been more swift in the process of his justice against the sins of a professing people. God may reprieve this land a while by prerogative, but if ever he save it without repentance, he must go out of his ordinary road.

I say therefore with Mr Bradford,[1] 'Repent, O England!' You have be-lepered[2] yourself with sin, and must needs go and wash in the spiritual Jordan. You have kindled God's anger against you. Throw away your weapons, and bring your holy engines and water-works, that God may be appeased in the blood of Christ. Let your tears run; let God's roll of curses fly (*Zech.* 5.2). Either men must turn or God will overturn. Either the fallow ground of their hearts must be broken up or the land broken down. If no words will prevail with sinners, it is because God has a purpose to slay them (*1 Sam.* 2.25). Among the Romans, it was concluded that he who for his capital offence was forbidden the use of water was a condemned person. So they who by their prodigious sins have so far incensed the God of heaven that he denies them the water of repentance may look upon themselves as condemned persons.

(3) Repentance is necessary for the cheating crew: 'their deceit is falsehood' (*Ps.* 119.118); 'they are wise to do evil' (*Jer.* 4.22), making use of their invention only for circumvention. Instead of living by their faith, they live by their shifts. These are they who make themselves poor so that by this artifice they may grow rich. I would not be misunderstood. I do not mean such as the providence of God has brought low, whose estates have failed but not their honesty, but rather such as feign a break, that they

---

[1] John Bradford, born in Manchester, was a leading Protestant reformer in the Reformation period. He was martyred by Queen Mary in 1555.

[2] The reference is obviously to the case of Naaman the leper (2 Kings 5).

may cheat their creditors. There are some who get more by breaking than others can by trading. These are like beggars that discolour and blister their arms that they may move charity. As they live by their sores, so these live by their breaking. When the frost breaks, the streets are more full of water. Likewise, many tradesmen, when they break, are fuller of money. These make as if they had nothing, but out of this nothing great estates are created. Remember, the kingdom of heaven is taken by force, not by fraud. Let men know that after this golden sop, the devil enters. They squeeze a curse into their estates. They must repent quickly. Though the bread of falsehood be sweet (*Prov. 20.17*), yet many vomit up their sweet morsels in hell.

(4) Repentance is necessary for civil persons. These have no visible spots on them. They are free from gross sin, and one would think they had nothing to do with the business of repentance. They are so good that they scorn a psalm of mercy. Indeed these are often in the worst condition: these are they who need no repentance (*Luke 15.7*). Their civility undoes them. They make a Christ of it, and so on this shelf they suffer shipwreck. Morality shoots short of heaven. It is only nature refined. A moral man is but old Adam dressed in fine clothes. The king's image counterfeited and stamped upon brass will not go current. The civil person seems to have the image of God, but he is only brass metal, which will never pass for current. Civility is insufficient for salvation. Though the life be moralized, the lust may be unmortified. The heart may be full of pride and atheism. Under the fair leaves of a tree there may be a worm. I am not saying, repent that you are civil, but that you are no more than civil. Satan entered into the house that had just been swept and garnished (*Luke 11.26*). This is the emblem of a moral man, who is swept by civility and garnished with

common gifts, but is not washed by true repentance. The unclean spirit enters into such a one. If civility were sufficient to salvation, Christ need not have died. The civilian has a fair lamp, but it lacks the oil of grace.

(5) Repentance is needful for hypocrites. I mean such as allow themselves in the sin. Hypocrisy is the counterfeiting of sanctity. The hypocrite or stage-player has gone a step beyond the moralist and dressed himself in the garb of religion. He pretends to a form of godliness but denies the power (2 *Tim. 3.5*). The hypocrite is a saint in jest. He makes a magnificent show, like an ape clothed in ermine or purple. The hypocrite is like a house with a beautiful façade, but every room within is dark. He is a rotten post fairly gilded. Under his mask of profession he hides his plague-sores. The hypocrite is against painting of faces, but he paints holiness. He is seemingly good so that he may be really bad. In Samuel's mantle he plays the devil. Therefore the same word in the original signifies to use hypocrisy and to be profane. The hypocrite seems to have his eyes nailed to heaven, but his heart is full of impure lustings. He lives in secret sin against his conscience. He can be as his company is and act both the dove and the vulture. He hears the word, but is *all ear*. He is for temple-devotion, where others may look upon him and admire him, but he neglects family and closet prayer. Indeed, if prayer does not make a man leave sin, sin will make him leave prayer. The hypocrite feigns humility, but it is that he may rise in the world. He is a pretender to faith, but he makes use of it rather for a cloak than a shield. He carries his Bible under his arm, but not in his heart. His whole religion is a demure lie (*Hos. 11.12*).

But is there such a generation of men to be found? The Lord forgive them their holiness! Hypocrites are 'in the gall of bitterness' (*Acts 8.23*). O how they need to humble themselves in the dust! They are far gone with the rot, and if any thing can cure them, it must be feeding upon the salt marshes of repentance.

Let me speak my mind freely. None will find it more difficult to repent than hypocrites. They have so juggled in religion that their treacherous hearts know not how to repent. Hypocrisy is harder to cure than frenzy. The hypocrite's imposthume in his heart seldom breaks. If it be not too late, seek yet to God for mercy.

Such as are guilty of prevailing hypocrisy, let them fear and tremble. Their condition is sinful and sad. It is sinful because they do not embrace religion out of choice but design; they do not love it, only paint it. It is sad upon a double account. Firstly, because this art of deceit cannot hold long; he who hangs out a sign but has not the commodity of grace in his heart must needs break at last. Secondly, because God's anger will fall heavier upon hypocrites. They dishonour God more and take away the gospel's good name. Therefore the Lord reserves the most deadly arrows in his quiver to shoot at them. If heathens be damned, hypocrites shall be double-damned. Hell is called the place of hypocrites (*Matt.* 24.51), as if it were chiefly prepared for them and were to be settled upon them in fee-simple.[1]

(6) Repentance is necessary for God's own people, who have a real work of grace and are Israelites indeed. They must offer up a daily sacrifice of tears. The Antinomians hold that when any come to be believers, they have a writ of ease, and there remains nothing for them now to do but to rejoice. Yes, they have something else to do, and that is to repent. Repentance is a continuous act. The issue of godly sorrow must not be quite stopped till death. Jerome, writing in an epistle to Laeta, tells her that her life must be a life of repentance.

[1] Unconditional inheritance

THE DOCTRINE OF REPENTANCE

Repentance is called crucifying the flesh (*Gal.* 5.24), which is not done on a sudden, but leisurely; it will be doing all our life.

And are there not many reasons why God's own people should go into the weeping bath? 'Are there not with you, even with you, sins against the Lord?' (*2 Chron.* 28.10). Have not you sins of daily incursion? Though you are diamonds, have you no flaws? Do we not read of the 'spot of God's children' (*Deut.* 32.5). Search with the candle of the word into your hearts and see if you can find no matter for repentance there.

(a) Repent of your rash censuring. Instead of praying for others, you are ready to pass a verdict upon them. It is true that the saints shall judge the world (*1 Cor.* 6.2), but stay your time; remember the apostle's caution in 1 Corinthians 4.5: 'judge nothing before the time, until the Lord come'.

(b) Repent of your vain thoughts. These swarm in your minds as the flies did in Pharaoh's court (*Exod.* 8.24). What bewilderings there are in the imagination! If Satan does not possess your bodies, he does your fancies. 'How long shall thy vain thoughts lodge within thee?' (*Jer.* 4.14). A man may think himself into hell. O ye saints, be humbled for this lightness in your head.

(c) Repent of your vain fashions. It is strange that the garments which God has given to cover shame should discover pride. The godly are bid not to be conformed to this world (*Rom.* 12.2). People of the world are garish and light in their dresses. It is in fashion nowadays to go to hell. But whatever others do, yet let not Judah offend (*Hos.* 4.15). The apostle Paul has set down what upper garment Christians must wear: 'modest apparel' (*1 Tim.* 2.9); and what under-garment: 'be clothed with humility' (*1 Pet.* 5.5).

(d) Repent of your decays in grace: 'thou hast left thy

first love' (*Rev. 2.4*). Christians, how often is it low water in your souls! How often does your cold fit come upon you! Where are those flames of affection, those sweet meltings of spirit that once you had? I fear they are melted away. Oh repent for leaving your first love!

(e) Repent of your non-improvement of talents. Health is a talent; estate is a talent; wit and parts are talents; and these God has entrusted you with to improve for his glory. He has sent you into the world as a merchant sends his factor beyond the seas to trade for his master's advantage, but you have not done the good you might. Can you say, 'Lord, thy pound hath gained five pounds' (*Luke 19.18*)? O mourn at the burial of your talents! Let it grieve you that so much of your age has not been time lived but time lost; that you have filled up your golden hours more with froth than with spirits.

(f) Repent of your forgetfulness of sacred vows. A vow is a binding one's soul to God (*Num. 30.2*). Christians, have not you, since you have been bound to God, forfeited your indentures? Have you not served for common uses after you have been the Lord's by solemn dedication? Thus, by breach of vows you have made a breach in your peace. Surely this calls for a fresh laver of tears.

(g) Repent of your unanswerableness to blessings received. You have lived all your life upon free quarter. You have spent your stock of free graces. You have been be-miracled with mercy. But where are your returns of love to God? The Athenians would have ungrateful persons sued at law. Christians, may not God sue you at law for your unthankfulness? 'I will recover my wool and my flax' (*Hos. 2.9*); I will recover them by law.

(h) Repent of your worldliness. By your profession you seem to resemble the birds of paradise that soar aloft and live upon the dew of heaven. Yet as serpents you lick the dust. Baruch, a good man, was taxed with this: 'seekest thou great things for thyself?' (*Jer. 45.5*).

(i) Repent of your divisions. These are a blot in your coat-armour and make others stand aloof from religion. Indeed, to separate from the wicked resembles Christ, who was 'separate from sinners' (*Heb. 7.26*), but for the godly to divide among themselves and look askew one upon another, had we as many eyes as there are stars, they were few enough to weep for this. Divisions eclipse the church's beauty and weaken her strength. God's Spirit brought in cloven tongues among the saints (*Acts 2.3*), but the devil has brought in cloven hearts. Surely this deserves a shower of tears:

Quis talia fando
Temperet a lachrymis?[1]

(j) Repent for the iniquity of your holy things. How often have the services of God's worship been frozen with formality and soured with pride? There have been more of the peacock's plumes than the groans of the dove. It is sad that ever duties of religion should be made a stage for vainglory to act upon. O Christians, there is such a thick rhyne[2] upon your duties that it is to be feared there is but little meat left in them for God to feed upon.

Behold here repenting work cut out for the best. And that which may make the tide of grief swell higher is to think that the sins of God's people do more provoke God than do the sins of others (*Deut. 32.19*). The sins of the wicked pierce Christ's side. The sins of the godly go to his heart. Peter's sin, being against so much love, was most unkind, which made his cheeks to be furrowed with tears: 'When he thought thereon, he wept' (*Mark 14.72*).

---

[1]'Whoever is sowing such things, can he refrain from tears?'
[2]Rind, crust.

3. *Repentance is necessary for all sins*

Let us be deeply humbled and mourn before the Lord for original sin. We have lost that pure quintessential frame of soul that once we had. Our nature is vitiated with corruption. Original sin has diffused itself as a poison into the whole man, like the Jerusalem artichoke which, wherever it is planted, soon overruns the ground. There are not worse natures in hell than we have. The hearts of the best are like Peter's sheet, on which there were a number of unclean creeping things (*Acts 10.12*). This primitive corruption is bitterly to be bewailed because we are never free from it. It is like a spring underground, which though it is not seen, yet it still runs. We may as well stop the beating of the pulse as stop the motions to sin.

This inbred depravity retards and hinders us in that which is spiritual: 'the good that I would I do not' (*Rom. 7.19*). Original sin may be compared to that fish Pliny[1] speaks of, a sea-lamprey, which cleaves to the keel of the ship and hinders it when it is under sail. Sin hangs weights upon us so that we move but slowly to heaven. O this adherence of sin! Paul shook the viper which was on his hand into the fire (*Acts 28.5*), but we cannot shake off original corruption in this life. Sin does not come as a lodger for a night, but as an indweller: 'sin that dwelleth in me' (*Rom. 7.17*). It is with us as with one who has a hectic fever upon him; though he changes the air, yet still he carries his disease with him. Original sin is inexhaustible. This ocean cannot be emptied. Though the stock of sin spends, yet it is not at all diminished. The more we sin, the fuller we are of sin. Original corruption is like the widow's oil which increased by pouring out.

Another wedge to break our hearts is that original sin mixes with the very habits of grace. Hence it is that our

---

[1] A Roman writer on natural history in the first century A.D.

actings towards heaven are so dull and languid. Why does faith act no stronger but because it is clogged with sense? Why does love to God burn no purer but because it is hindered with lust? Original sin incorporates with our graces. As bad lungs cause an asthma or shortness of breath, so original sin having infected our heart, our graces breathe now very faintly. Thus we see what in original sin may draw forth our tears.

In particular, let us lament the corruption of our will and our affections. Let us mourn for the corruption of our will. The will not following the dictamen[1] of right reason is biased to evil. The will distasts[2] God, not as he is good, but as he is holy. It contumaciously affronts him: 'we will do whatsoever goeth forth out of our own mouth, to burn incense unto the queen of heaven' (*Jer.* 44.17). The greatest wound has fallen upon our will.

Let us grieve for the diversion of our affections. They are taken off from their proper object. The affections, like arrows, shoot beside the mark. At the beginning our affections were wings to fly to God; now they are weights to pull us from him.

Let us grieve for the inclination of our affections. Our love is set on sin, our joy on the creature. Our affections, like the lapwing, feed on dung. How justly may the distemper of our affections bear a part in the scene of our grief? We of ourselves are falling into hell, and our affections would thrust us thither.

Let us lay to heart actual sins. Of these I may say, 'Who can understand his errors?' (*Ps.* 19.12). They are like atoms in the sun, like sparks of a furnace. We have sinned in our eyes; they have been casements to let in vanity. We have sinned in our tongues; they have been fired with

[1]Precept, injunction
[2]Dislikes.

passion. What action proceeds from us wherein we do not betray some sin? To reckon up these were to go to number the drops in the ocean. Let actual sins be solemnly repented of before the Lord.

Chapter Seven

POWERFUL MOTIVES TO REPENTANCE

That the exhortation to repentance may be more quickened, I shall lay down some powerful motives to excite repentance.

1. *Sorrow and melting of heart fits us for every holy duty*

A piece of lead, while it is in the lump, can be put to no use, but melt it, and you may then cast it into any mould, and it is made useful. So a heart that is hardened into a lump of sin is good for nothing, but when it is dissolved by repentance, it is useful. A melting heart is fit to pray. When Paul's heart was humbled and melted, then 'behold, he prayeth' (*Acts 9.11*). It is fit to hear the word. Now the word works kindly. When Josiah's heart was tender, he humbled himself and rent his clothes at the hearing of the words of the law (2 *Chron. 34.19*). His heart, like melting wax, was ready to take any seal of the word. A melting heart is fit to obey. When the heart is like metal in the furnace, it is facile and malleable to anything: 'Lord, what wilt thou have me to do?' (*Acts 9.6*). A repenting soul subscribes to God's will and answers to his call, as the echo to the voice.

2. *Repentance is highly acceptable*

When a spiritual river runs to water this garden, then our hearts are a garden of Eden, delightful to God. I have read that doves delight to be about the waters. And surely God's Spirit, who descended in the likeness of a dove, takes great delight in the waters of repentance

The Lord esteems no heart sound but the broken heart: 'The sacrifices of God are a broken spirit' (*Ps. 51.17*). Mary stood at Jesus' feet weeping (*Luke 7.38*). She brought two things to Christ, said Augustine, *unguentum* and *lachrymas* (ointment and tears). Her tears were better than her ointment. Tears are powerful orators for mercy. They are silent, yet they have a voice: 'the Lord hath heard the voice of my weeping' (*Ps. 6.8*).

3. *Repentance commends all our services to God*

That which is seasoned with the bitter herbs of godly sorrow is God's savoury meat. Hearing of the word is then good, when we are pricked at the heart (*Acts 2.37*). Prayer is delightful to God when it ascends from the altar of a broken heart. The publican smote upon his breast saying, 'God be merciful to me a sinner'. This prayer pierced heaven: 'he went away justified rather than the other' (*Luke 18.14*). No prayer touches God's ear but what comes from a heart touched with the sense of sin.

4. *Without repentance nothing will avail us*

Some bless themselves that they have a stock of knowledge, but what is knowledge good for without repentance? It is better to mortify one sin than to understand all mysteries. Impure speculatists do but resemble Satan transformed into an angel of light. Learning and a bad heart is like a fair face with a cancer in the breast. Knowledge without repentance will be but a torch to light men to hell.

5. *Repenting tears are delicious*

They may be compared to myrrh, which though it is bitter in taste has a sweet smell and refreshes the spirits. So repentance, though it is bitter in itself, yet it is sweet in the effects. It bring inward peace. The soul is never more enlarged and inwardly delighted than when it can kindly melt. Alexander,[1] upon the safe return of his admiral Nearchus from a long voyage, wept for joy. How oft do the saints fall a-weeping for joy! The Hebrew word for 'repent' signifies 'to take comfort'. None so joyful as the penitent! Tears, as the philosopher notes, have four qualities: they are moist, salt, hot, and bitter. It is true of repenting tears. They are hot, to warm a frozen conscience; moist, to soften a hard heart; salt, to season a soul putrifying in sin; bitter, to wean us from the love of the world. And I will add a fifth. They are sweet, in that they make the heart inwardly rejoice: 'and sorrow shall be turned into joy' (*Job* 41.22). Let a man, said Augustine, grieve for his sin and rejoice for his grief. Tears are the best sweetmeats. David, who was the great weeper in Israel, was the sweet singer of Israel. The sorrows of the penitent are like the sorrows of a travailing woman: 'A woman when she is in travail hath sorrow, but as soon as she is delivered of the child, she remembereth no more the anguish, for joy that a man is born into the world' (*John* 16.21). So the sorrows of humbled sinners bring forth grace, and what joy there is when this man-child is born!

6. *Great sins repented of shall find mercy*

Mary Magdalene, a great sinner, obtained pardon when she washed Christ's feet with her tears. For some of the Jews who had a hand in crucifying Christ, upon their repentance, the very blood they shed was a sovereign balm to heal them: 'though your sins be as scarlet, they shall be as white as snow' (*Isa. 1.18*). Scarlet in the Greek is called 'dibasson', because it is 'twice dipped', and the art of man cannot wash out the dye again. But though our sins are of a scarlet colour, God's mercy can wash them

---

[1] Alexander the Great of Macedonia (356–323 B.C.). When Alexander's conquests reached as far as India, he required Nearchus to explore the Indian Ocean.

away. This may comfort those whom the heinousness of their sin discourages, as if there were no hope for them. Yes, upon their serious turning to God, their sins shall be expunged and done away with.

Oh, but my sins are out of measure sinful! Do not make them greater by not repenting. Repentance unravels sin and makes it as if it had never been.

Oh, but I have relapsed into sin after pardon, and surely there is no mercy for me! I know the Novatians[1] held that after a lapse there was no renewing by repentance; but doubtless that was an error. The children of God have relapsed into the same sin: Abraham did twice equivocate; Lot committed incest twice; Asa, a good king, yet sinned twice by creature-confidence, and Peter twice by carnal fear (*Matt. 26.70; Gal. 2.12*). But for the comfort of such as have relapsed into sin more than once, if they solemnly repent, a white flag of mercy shall be held forth to them. Christ commands us to forgive our trespassing brother seventy times seven in one day, in case he repents (*Matt. 18.22*). If the Lord bids us do it, will not he be much more ready to forgive upon our repentance? What is our forgiving mercy to his? This I speak not to encourage any impenitent sinner, but to comfort a despondent sinner that thinks it is in vain for him to repent and that he is excluded from mercy.

7. *Repentance is the inlet to spiritual blessings*

It helps to enrich us with grace. It causes the desert to blossom as the rose. It makes the soul as the Egyptian fields after the overflowing of the Nile, flourishing and fruitful. Never do the flowers of grace grow more than after a shower of repentant tears. Repentance causes knowledge: 'When their heart shall turn to the Lord, the

---

[1] An extreme Christian group of the third century who were noted for their severity to Christians who stumbled and fell.

veil shall be taken away' (2 *Cor.* 3.16). The veil of ignorance which was drawn over the Jews' eyes shall by repentance be taken away. Repentance inflames love. Weeping Mary Magdalene loved much (*Luke* 7.47). God preserves these springs of sorrow in the soul to water the fruit of the Spirit (*Gal.* 5.22).

8. *Repentance ushers in temporal blessings*

The prophet Joel, persuading the people to repentance, brings in the promise of secular good things: 'rend your heart, and not your garments, and turn unto the Lord . . . the Lord will answer and say to his people, Behold, I will send you corn, and wine, and oil' (*Joel* 2.13,19). When we put water into the pump, it fetches up only water, but when we put the water of tears into God's bottle, this fetches up wine: 'I will send you wine, and oil'. Sin blasts the fruits of the earth: 'Ye have sown much, and bring in little' (*Hag.* 1.6). But repentance makes the pomegranate bud and the vine flourish with full clusters. Fill God's bottle, and he will fill your basket. 'If thou return to the Almighty, thou shalt lay up gold as dust' (*Job* 22.23–4). Repenting is a returning to God, and this brings a golden harvest.

9. *Repentance staves off judgments from a land*

When God is going to destroy a nation, the penitent sinner stays his hand, as the angel did Abraham's (*Gen.* 22.12). The Ninevites' repentance caused God to repent: 'God saw that they turned from their evil way; and God repented of the evil, that he had said that he would do unto them; and he did it not' (*Jon.* 3.10). An outward repentance has adjourned and kept off wrath. Ahab sold himself to work wickedness; yet upon his fasting and rending his garments, God said to Elijah, 'I will not bring the evil in his days' (*1 Kings* 21.29). If the rending of the clothes kept off judgment from the nation, what will the rending of the heart do?

10. *Repentance makes joy in heaven*

The angels do, as it were, keep holy day: 'There is joy in the presence of the angels of God over one sinner that repenteth' (*Luke 15.10*). As praise is the music of heaven, so repentance is the joy of heaven. When men neglect the offer of salvation and freeze in sin, this delights the devils, but when a soul is brought home to Christ by repentance this makes joy among the angels.

11. *Consider how dear our sins cost Christ*

To consider how dear our sins cost Christ may cause tears to distil from our eyes. Christ is called the Rock (*1 Cor. 10.4*). When his hands were pierced with nails, and the spear thrust in his side, then was this Rock smitten, and there came out water and blood. And all this Christ endured for us: 'the Messiah shall be cut off, but not for himself' (*Dan. 9.26*). We tasted the apple, and he the vinegar and gall. We sinned in every faculty, and he bled in every vein: *Cernis ut in toto corpore sculptus amor.*[1]

Can we look upon a suffering Saviour with dry eyes? Shall we not be sorry for those sins which made Christ a man of sorrow? Shall not our enormities, which drew blood from Christ, draw tears from us? Shall we sport any more with sin and so rake in Christ's wounds? Oh that by repentance we could crucify our sins afresh! The Jews said to Pilate, 'If thou let this man go, thou art not Caesar's friend' (*John 19.12*). If we let our sins go and do not crucify them, we are not Christ's friends.

12. *This is the end of all afflictions which God sends*, whether it be sickness in our bodies or losses in our estates, that he may awaken us out of our sins and make the waters of repentance flow. Why did God lead Israel that march in the wilderness among fiery serpents but

[1] 'Flesh like love engraved on the whole body.'

that he might humble them (*Deut. 8.2*)? Why did he bring Manasseh so low, changing his crown of gold into fetters of iron but that he might learn repentance? 'He humbled himself greatly before the God of his fathers . . . Then Manasseh knew that the Lord he was God' (*2 Chron. 33.12,13*). One of the best ways to cure a man of his lethargy is to cast him into a fever. Likewise when a person is stupified and his conscience grown lethargical, God, to cure him of this distemper, puts him to extremity and brings one burning calamity or another, that he may startle him out of his security and make him return to him by repentance.

13. *The days of our mourning will soon be ended*

After a few showers that fall from our eyes, we shall have perpetual sunshine. Christ will provide a hand-kerchief to wipe off his people's tears: 'God shall wipe away all tears' (*Rev. 7.17*). Christians, you will shortly put on your garments of praise. You will exchange your sackcloth for white robes. Instead of sighs you will have triumphs, instead of groans, anthems, instead of the water of tears, the water of life. The mourning of the dove will be past, and the time of the singing of birds will come. *Volitant super aethera cantus.*[1] This brings me to the next point.

14. *The happy and glorious reward that follows upon repentance*

'Being made free from sin, ye have your fruit unto holiness, and the end everlasting life' (*Rom. 6.22*). The leaves and root of the fig-tree are bitter, but the fruit is sweet. Repentance to the fleshy part seems bitter, but behold sweet fruit: everlasting life. The Turks fancy after this life an Elysium or paradise of pleasure, where dainty dishes will be served in, and they will have gold in

---

[1]'Songs fly to and fro above the heavens.'

abundance, silken and purple apparel, and angels will bring them red wine in silver cups, and golden plates. Here is an epicure's heaven. But in the true paradise of God there are astonishing delights and rare viands served in, which 'eye hath not seen, neither have entered into the heart of man' (*1 Cor.* 2.9). God will lead his penitents from the house of mourning to the banqueting house. There will be no sight there but of glory, no noise but of music, no sickness unless of love. There shall be holiness unspotted and joy unspeakable. Then the saints shall forget their solitary hours and be sweetly solacing themselves in God and bathing in the rivers of divine pleasure.

O Christian, what are your duties compared with the recompense of reward? What an infinite disproportion is there between repentance enjoined and glory prepared? There was a feast-day at Rome, when they used to crown their fountains. God will crown those heads which have been fountains of tears. Who would not be willing to be a while in the house of mourning who shall be possessed of such glory as put Peter and John into an ecstasy to see it even darkly, shadowed and portrayed in the transfiguration (*Matt.* 17)? This reward which free grace gives is so transcendently great that could we have but a glimpse of glory revealed to us here, we should need patience to be content to live any longer. O blessed repentance, that has such a light side with the dark, and has so much sugar at the bottom of the bitter cup!

15. *The next motive to repentance is to consider the evil of impenitence*

A hard heart is the worst heart. It is called a heart of stone (*Ezek.* 36.26). If it were iron it might be mollified in the furnace, but a stone put in the fire will not melt; it will sooner fly in your face. Impenitence is a sin that grieves Christ: 'being grieved for the hardness of their hearts'

(*Mark* 3.5). It is not so much the disease that offends the physician as the contempt of his physic. It is not so much the sins we have committed that so provoke and grieve Christ as that we refuse the physic of repentance which he prescribes. This aggravated Jezebel's sin: 'I gave her space to repent, and she repented not' (*Rev*. 2.21). A hard heart receives no impression. It is untuned for every duty. It was a sad speech Stephen Gardiner[1] uttered on his death-bed: 'I have denied my Master with Peter, but I cannot repent with Peter.' Oh the plague of an obdurate heart! Pharaoh's heart turned into stone was worse than his waters turned into blood. David had his choice of three judgments – plague, sword, and famine – but he would have chosen them all rather than a hard heart. An impenitent sinner is neither allured by entreaties nor affrighted by menaces. Such as will not weep with Peter shall weep like Judas. A hard heart is the anvil on which the hammer of God's justice will be striking to all eternity.

16. *The last motive to repentance is that the day of judgment is coming*

This is the apostle's own argument: 'God commands all men every where to repent; because he hath appointed a day, in the which he will judge the world' (*Acts* 17.30–1). There is that in the day of judgment which may make a stony heart bleed. Will a man go on thieving when the assizes are nigh? Will the sinner go on sinning when the day of judgment is so nigh? You can no more conceal your sin than you can defend it. And what will you do when all your sins shall be written in God's book and engraven on your forehead? O direful day, when Jesus Christ, clothed in his judge's robe, shall say to the sinner,

[1]Roman Catholic bishop, a chief opponent of the Reformation of the sixteenth century. He urged the re-introduction of laws for the burning of Protestants.

'Stand forth; answer to the indictment brought against you. What can you say for all your oaths, adulteries, and your desperate impenitence?' O how amazed and stricken with consternation will the sinner be! And after his conviction he must hear the sad sentence, 'Depart from me!' Then, he that would not repent of his sins shall repent of his folly. If there be such a time coming, wherein God will judge men for their impieties, what a spur should this be to repentance! The penitent soul shall at the last day lift up his head with comfort and have a discharge to show under the Judge's own hand.

Chapter Eight

EXHORTATIONS TO SPEEDY REPENTANCE

The second branch of the exhortation is to press persons to speedy repentance: 'now God commandeth all men every where to repent' (*Acts 17.30*). The Lord would not have any of the late autumn fruits offered to him. God loves early penitents that consecrate the spring and flower of their age to him. Early tears, like pearls bred of the morning dew, are more orient and beautiful. O do not reserve the dregs of your age for God, lest he reserve the dregs of his cup for you! Be as speedy in your repentance as you would have God speedy in his mercies: 'the king's business required haste' (*1 Sam. 21.8*). Therefore repentance requires haste.

It is natural to us to procrastinate and put off repentance. We say, as Haggai did, 'The time is not come' (*Hag. 1.2*). No man is so bad but he purposes to amend, but he adjourns and prorogues so long, until at last all his purposes prove abortive. Many are now in hell that purposed to repent. Satan does what he can to keep men from repentance. When he sees that they begin to take up serious thoughts of reformation, he bids them wait a little longer. If this traitor, sin, must die (says Satan), let it not die yet. So the devil gets a reprieve for sin; it shall not die this sessions. At last men put off so long that death seizes on them, and their work is not done. Let me therefore lay down some cogent arguments to persuade to speedy repentance:

1. *Now is the season of repentance, and everything is best done in its season*

'Now is the accepted time' (2 *Cor.* 6.2); now God has a mind to show mercy to the penitent. He is on the giving hand. Kings set apart days for healing. Now is the healing day for our souls. Now God hangs forth the white flag and is willing to parley with sinners. A prince at his coronation, as an act of royalty, gives money, proclaims pardons, fills the conduits with wine. Now God promises pardons to penitent sinners. Now the conduit of the gospel runs wine. Now is the accepted time. Therefore come in now and make your peace with God. Break off your iniquities now by repentance. It is wisdom to take the season. The husbandman takes the season for sowing his seed. Now is the seed-time for our souls.

2. *The sooner you repent the fewer sins you will have to answer for*

At the death-bed of an old sinner, where conscience begins to be awakened, you will hear him crying out: here are all my old sins come about me, haunting my death-bed as so many evil spirits, and I have no discharge; here is Satan, who was once my tempter, now become an accuser, and I have no advocate; I am now going to be dragged before God's judgment-seat where I must receive my final doom! O how dismal is the case of this man. He is in hell before his time! But you who repent betimes of your sinful courses, this is your privilege: you will have the less to answer for. Indeed, let me tell you, you will have nothing to answer for. Christ will answer for you. Your judge will be your advocate (*1 John* 2.*1*). Father, Christ will say, here is one that has been a great sinner, yet a broken-hearted sinner; if he owes anything to your justice, set it on my score.

3. *The sooner we repent, the more glory we may bring to God*

It is the end of our living, to be useful in our generation. Better lose our lives than the end of our living. Late converts who have for many years taken pay on the devil's side are not in a capacity of doing so much work in the vineyard. The thief on the cross could not do that service for God as St Paul did. But when we do betimes turn from sin, then we give God the first-fruits of our lives. We spend and are spent for Christ. The more work we do for God, the more willing we shall be to die, and the sweeter death will be. He that has wrought hard at his day-labour is willing to go to rest at night. Such as have been honouring God all their lives, how sweetly will they sleep in the grave! The more work we do for God, the greater will our reward be. He whose pound had gained ten pounds, Christ did not only commend him, but advance him: 'have thou authority over ten cities' (*Luke* *19.17*). By late repentance, though we do not lose our crown, yet we make it lighter.

4. *It is of dangerous consequence to put off repentance longer*

Mora trahit periculum[1] It is dangerous, if we consider what sin is: sin is a poison. It is dangerous to let poison lie long in the body. Sin is a bruise. If a bruise be not soon cured, it gangrenes and kills. If sin be not soon cured by repentance it festers the conscience and damns. Why should any love to dwell in the tents of wickedness? They are under the power of Satan (*Acts* *26.18*), and it is dangerous to stay long in the enemy's quarters.

It is dangerous to procrastinate repentance because the longer any go on in sin the harder they will find the work of repentance. Delay strengthens sin and hardens the heart and gives the devil fuller possession. A plant at first may be easily plucked up, but when it has spread its roots

[1]'Procrastination brings dangers.'

deep in the earth, a whole team cannot remove it. It is hard to remove sin when once it comes to be rooted. The longer the ice freezes the harder it is to be broken. The longer a man freezes in security, the harder it will be to have his heart broken. The longer any travail with iniquity the sharper pangs they must expect in the new birth. When sin has got a haunt it is not easily shaken off. Sin comes to a sinner as the elder brother came to his father: 'Lo, these many years do I serve thee, neither transgressed I at any time thy commandment' (*Luke* 15.29), and wilt thou cast me off now? What, in my old age, after you have had so much pleasure by me? See how sin pleads custom, and that is a leopard's spot (*Jer.* 13.23).

It is dangerous to prorogue and delay repentance because there are three days that may soon expire:

(1) The day of the gospel may expire. This is a sunshiny day. It is sweet but swift. Jerusalem had a day but lost it: 'but now they are hid from thine eyes' (*Luke* 19.42). The Asian churches had a day, but at last the golden candlestick was removed. It would be a sad time in England to see the glory departed. With what hearts could we follow the gospel to the grave? To lose the gospel were far worse than to have our city charter taken from us. 'Gray hairs are here and there' (*Hos.* 7.9). I will not say the sun of the gospel is set in England, but I am sure it is under a cloud. That was a sad speech, 'The kingdom of God shall be taken from you' (*Matt.* 21.43). Therefore it is dangerous to delay repentance, lest the market of the gospel should remove and the vision cease.

(2) A man's personal day of grace may expire. What if that time should come when God should say the means of grace shall do no good: ordinances shall have 'a miscarrying womb and dry breasts' (*Hos.* 9.14)? Were it not

sad to adjourn repentance till such a decree came forth? It is true, no man can justly tell that his day of grace is past, but there are two shrewd signs by which he may fear it:

(a) When conscience has done preaching. Conscience is a bosom-preacher. Sometimes it convinces, sometimes it reproves. It says, as Nathan to David, 'Thou art the man' (2 Sam. 12.7). But men imprison this preacher, and God says to conscience, Preach no more: 'he which is filthy, let him be filthy still!' (Rev. 22.11). This is a fatal sign that a man's day of grace is past.

(b) When a person is in such a spiritual lethargy that nothing will work upon him or make him sensible. There is 'the spirit of deep sleep poured out upon you' (Isa. 29.10). This is a sad presage that his day of grace is past. How dangerous then is it to delay repentance when the day of grace may so soon expire!

(3) The day of life may expire. What security have we that we shall live another day? We are marching apace out of the world. We are going off the stage. Our life is a taper soon blown out. Man's life is compared to the flower of the field which withers sooner than the grass (Ps. 103.15). Our age is as nothing (Ps. 39.5). Life is but a flying shadow. The body is like a vessel filled with a little breath. Sickness broaches this vessel; death draws it out. O how soon may the scene alter! Many a virgin has been dressed the same day in her bride-apparel and her winding-sheet! How dangerous then is it to adjourn repenting when death may so suddenly make a thrust at us. Say not that you will repent tomorrow. Remember that speech of Aquinas[1]: God who pardons him that repents has not promised to give him tomorrow to repent in. I have read of Archias, a Lacedaemonian,[2] who was

---

[1]Thomas Aquinas (thirteenth century), one of the most famous of Roman Catholic theologians.

[2]An early name for Sparta in southern Greece.

among his cups, when one delivered him a letter and desired him to read the letter presently, which was of serious business. He replied, '*seria cras*' ('I will mind serious things tomorrow'); and that day he was slain. Thus while men think to spin out their silver thread, death cuts it. Olaus Magnus[1] observes of the birds of Norway that they fly faster than the birds of any other country. Not that their wings are swifter than others, but by an instinct of nature they, knowing the days in that climate to be very short, not above three hours long, do therefore make the more haste to their nests. So we, knowing the shortness of our lives and how quickly we may be called away by death, should fly so much the faster on the wing of repentance to heaven.

But some will say that they do not fear a sudden surprisal; they will repent upon their sick-bed. I do not much like a sick-bed repentance. He who will venture his salvation within the circle of a few short minutes runs a desperate hazard. You who put off repentance till sickness, answer me to these four queries:

(a) How do you know that you shall have a time of sickness? Death does not always shoot its warning-piece by a lingering consumption. Some it arrests suddenly. What if God should presently send you a summons to surrender your life?

(b) Suppose you should have a time of sickness, how do you know that you shall have the use of your senses? Many are distracted on their sick-bed.

(c) Suppose you should have your senses, yet how do you know your mind will be in a frame for such a work as repentance? Sickness does so discompose body and mind that one is but in an ill posture at such a time to take care for his soul. In sickness a man is scarce fit to make his will,

---

[1] A sixteenth century Swedish ecclesiastic who wrote on Scandinavian customs and folklore.

THE DOCTRINE OF REPENTANCE

much less to make his peace. The apostle said, 'Is any sick among you? let him call for the elders of the church' (*James 5.14*). He does not say, Is he sick? let him pray, but let him call for the elders that they may pray over him'. A sick man is very unfit to pray or repent; he is likely to make but sick work of it. When the body is out of tune, the soul must needs jar in its devotion. Upon a sick bed a person is more fit to exercise impatience than repentance. We read that at the pouring out of the fourth vial, when God did smite the inhabitants and scorched them with fire, that 'they blasphemed the name of God, and repented not' (*Rev. 16.9*). So when the Lord pours out his vial and scorches the body with a fever, the sinner is fitter to blaspheme than to repent.

(d) How do you who put off all to a sick-bed know that God will give you in that very juncture of time grace to repent? The Lord usually punishes neglect of repentance in time of health with hardness of heart in time of sickness. You have in your lifetime repulsed the Spirit of God, and are you sure he will come at your call? You have not taken the first season, and perhaps you shall never see another spring-tide of the Spirit again. All this considered may hasten our repentance. Do not lay too much weight upon a sick-bed. 'Do thy diligence to come before winter' (*2 Tim. 4.21*). There is a winter of sickness and death a-coming. Therefore make haste to repent. Let your work be ready before winter. 'Today hear God's voice' (*Heb. 3.7*).

Chapter Nine

THE TRIAL OF OUR REPENTANCE, AND COMFORT FOR THE PENITENT

If any shall say they have repented, let me desire them to try themselves seriously by those seven adjuncts or effects of repentance which the apostle lays down in 2 Corinthians 7.11:

1. *Carefulness*

The Greek word signifies a solicitous diligence or careful shunning all temptations to sin. The true penitent flies from sin as Moses did from the serpent.

2. *Clearing of ourselves*

The Greek word is 'apology'. The sense is this: though we have much care, yet through strength of temptation we may slip into sin. Now in this case the repenting soul will not let sin lie festering in his conscience but judges himself for his sin. He pours out tears before the Lord. He begs mercy in the name of Christ and never leaves till he has gotten his pardon. Here he is cleared of guilt in his conscience and is able to make an apology for himself against Satan.

3. *Indignation*

He that repents of sin, his spirit rises against it, as one's blood rises at the sight of him whom he mortally hates. Indignation is a being fretted at the heart with sin. The penitent is vexed with himself. David calls himself a fool and a beast (*Ps.* 73.22). God is never better pleased with us than when we fall out with ourselves for sin.

4. Fear

A tender heart is ever a trembling heart. The penitent has felt sin's bitterness. This hornet has stung him and now, having hopes that God is reconciled, he is afraid to come near sin any more. The repenting soul is full of fear. He is afraid to lose God's favour which is better than life. He is afraid he should, for want of diligence, come short of salvation. He is afraid lest, after his heart has been soft, the waters of repentance should freeze and he should harden in sin again. 'Happy is the man that feareth alway' (Prov. 28.14). A sinner is like the leviathan who is made without fear (Job 41.33). A repenting person fears and sins not; a graceless person sins and fears not.

5. Vehement desire

As sour sauce sharpens the appetite, so the bitter herbs of repentance sharpen desire. But what does the penitent desire? He desires more power against sin and to be released from it. It is true, he has got loose from Satan, but he goes as a prisoner that has broken out of prison, with a fetter on his leg. He cannot walk with that freedom and swiftness in the ways of God. He desires therefore to have the fetters of sin taken off. He would be freed from corruption. He cries out with Paul: 'who shall deliver me from the body of this death?' (Rom. 7.24). In short, he desires to be with Christ, as everything desires to be in its centre.

6. Zeal

Desire and zeal are fitly put together to show that true desire puts forth itself in zealous endeavour. How does the penitent bestir himself in the business of salvation! How does he take the kingdom of heaven by force (Matt. 11.12)! Zeal quickens the pursuit after glory. Zeal, encountering difficulty, is emboldened by opposition and tramples upon danger. Zeal makes a repenting soul persist in godly sorrow against all discouragements and oppositions whatsoever. Zeal carries a man above himself for God's glory. Paul before conversion was mad against the saints (*Acts* 26.11), and after conversion he was judged mad for Christ's sake: 'Paul, thou art beside thyself' (*Acts* 26.24). But it was zeal, not frenzy. Zeal animates spirit and duty. It causes fervency in religion, which is as fire to the sacrifice (*Rom.* 12.11). As fear is a bridle to sin, so zeal is a spur to duty.

7. *Revenge*

A true penitent pursues his sins with a holy malice. He seeks the death of them as Samson was avenged on the Philistines for his two eyes. He uses his sins as the Jews used Christ. He gives them gall and vinegar to drink. He crucifies his lusts (*Gal.* 5.24). A true child of God seeks to be revenged most of those sins which have dishonoured God most. Cranmer, who had with his right hand subscribed the popish articles, was revenged on himself; he put his right hand first into the fire.[1] David did by sin defile his bed; afterwards by repentance he watered his bed with tears. Israel had sinned by idolatry, and afterwards they did offer disgrace to their idols: 'Ye shall defile also the covering of thy graven images of silver' (*Isa.* 30.22). Mary Magdalene had sinned in her eye by adulterous glances, and now she will be revenged on her eyes. She washes Christ's feet with her tears. She had sinned in her hair. It had entangled her lovers. Now she will be revenged on her hair; she wipes the Lord's feet with it. The Israelite women who had been dressing themselves by the hour and had abused their looking-glasses to pride, afterwards by way of revenge as well as zeal, offered their looking-glasses to the use and service of God's tabernacle (*Exod.* 38.8). So those conjurers who used curious arts or magic (as it is in the Syriac), when once they repented, brought their books and, by way of revenge, burned them (*Acts* 19.19).

---

[1] This happened as he was burned at the stake in Oxford in 1536.

These are the blessed fruits and products of repentance, and if we can find these in our souls we have arrived at that repentance which is never to be repented of (2 *Cor. 7.10*).

A Necessary Caution

Such as have solemnly repented of their sins, let me speak to them by way of caution. Though repentance be so necessary and excellent, as you have heard, yet take heed that you do not ascribe too much to repentance. The papists are guilty of a double error:

(1) They make repentance a sacrament. Christ never made it so. And who may institute sacraments but he who can give virtue to them? Repentance can be no sacrament because it lacks an outward sign. A sacrament cannot properly be without a sign.

(2) The papists make repentance meritorious. They say it does *ex congruo* (altogether fittingly) merit pardon. This is a gross error. Indeed repentance fits us for mercy. As the plough, when it breaks up the ground, fits it for the seed, so when the heart is broken up by repentance, it is fitted for remission, but it does not merit it. God will not save us without repentance, nor yet for it. Repentance is a qualification, not a cause. I grant repenting tears are precious. They are, as Gregory said, the fat of the sacrifice; as Basil[1] said, the medicine of the soul; and as Bernard,[2] the wine of angels. But yet, tears are not satisfactory for sin. We drop sin with our tears, therefore they cannot satisfy. Augustine said well: I have read of Peter's tears, but no man ever read of Peter's satisfaction. Christ's blood only can merit pardon. We please God by

[1] Basil the Great, one of the Fathers (fourth century).
[2] Bernard of Clairvaux (twelfth century).

repentance but we do not satisfy him by it. To trust to our repentance is to make it a saviour. Though repentance helps to purge out the filth of sin, yet it is Christ's blood that washes away the guilt of sin. Therefore do not idolize repentance. Do not rest upon this, that your heart has been wounded for sin, but rather that your Saviour has been wounded for sin. When you have wept, say with him: Lord Jesus, wash my tears in thy blood.

Comfort for the Repenting Sinner

Let me in the next place speak by way of comfort. Christian, has God given you a repenting heart? Know these three things for your everlasting comfort:

1. *Your sins are pardoned*

Pardon of sin circumscribes blessedness within it. (*Ps. 32.1*). Whom God pardons he crowns: 'who forgiveth all thine iniquities, who crowneth thee with lovingkindness' (*Ps. 103.3–4*). A repenting condition is a pardoned condition. Christ said to that weeping woman, 'Thy sins, which are many, are forgiven' (*Luke 7.47*). Pardons are sealed upon soft hearts. O you whose head has been a fountain to weep for sin, Christ's side will be a fountain to wash away sin (*Zech. 13.1*). Have you repented? God looks upon you as if you had not offended. He becomes a friend, a father. He will now bring forth the best robe and put it on you. God is pacified towards you and will, with the father of the prodigal, fall upon your neck and kiss you. Sin in scripture is compared to a cloud (*Is. 44.22*). No sooner is this cloud scattered by repentance than pardoning love shines forth. Paul, after his repentance, obtained mercy: 'I was all bestrowed with mercy' (*1 Tim. 1.16*). When a spring of repentance is open in the heart, a spring of mercy is open in heaven.

2. *God will pass an act of oblivion*

He so forgives sin as he forgets: 'I will remember their sin no more' (*Jer. 31.34*). Have you been penitentially humbled? The Lord will never upbraid you with your former sins. After Peter wept we never read that Christ upbraided him with his denial of him. God has cast your sins into the depths of the sea (*Mic. 7.19*). How? Not as cork, but as lead. The Lord will never in a judicial way account for them. When he pardons, God is as a creditor that blots the debt out of his book (*Isa. 43.25*). Some ask the question, whether the sins of the godly shall be mentioned at the last day. The Lord said he will not remember them, and he is blotting them out, so if their sins are mentioned, it shall not be to their prejudice, for the debt-book is crossed.

3. *Conscience will now speak peace*

O the music of conscience! Conscience is turned into a paradise, and there a Christian sweetly solaces himself and plucks the flowers of joy (*2 Cor. 1.12*). The repenting sinner can go to God with boldness in prayer and look upon him not as a judge, but as a father. He is 'born of God' and is heir to a kingdom (*Luke 6.20*). He is encircled with promises. He no sooner shakes the tree of the promise but some fruit falls.

To conclude, the true penitent may look on death with comfort. His life has been a life of tears, and now at death all tears shall be wiped away. Death shall not be a destruction, but a deliverance from gaol. Thus you see what great comfort remains for repenting sinners. Luther said that before his conversion he could not endure that bitter word 'repentance', but afterwards he found much sweetness in it.

Chapter Ten

THE REMOVING OF THE IMPEDIMENTS TO REPENTANCE

Before I lay down the expedients and means conducive to repentance, I shall first remove the impediments. In this great city,[1] when you lack water, you search the cause, whether the pipes are broken or stopped, that the current of water is hindered. Likewise when no water of repentance comes (though we have the conduit-pipes of ordinances), see what the cause is. What is the obstruction that these penitential waters do not run?

There are ten impediments to repentance:

1. *Men do not apprehend that they need repentance*
They thank God that all is well with them, and they know nothing they should repent of: 'thou sayest, I am rich, and have need of nothing' (*Rev. 3.17*). He who apprehends not any distemper in his body will not take the physic prescribed. This is the mischief sin has done; it has not only made us sick, but senseless. When the Lord bade the people return to him, they answered stubbornly, 'Wherein shall we return?' (*Mal. 3.7*). So when God bids men repent, they say, Wherefore should we repent? They know nothing they have done amiss. There is surely no disease worse than that which is apoplectical.[2]

2. *People conceive it an easy thing to repent*
It is but saying a few prayers: a sigh, or a 'Lord have

[1]London.
[2]Apoplexy is a malady, sudden in its attack, which arrests the powers of sense and motion.

mercy', and the work is done. This conceit of the easiness of repentance is a great hindrance to it. That which makes a person bold and adventurous in sin must needs obstruct repentance. This opinion makes a person bold in sin. The angler can let out his line as far as he will and then pull it in again. Likewise when a man thinks he can lash out in sin as far as he will and then pull in by repentance when he pleases, this must needs embolden him in wickedness. But to take away this false conceit of the easiness of repentance, consider:

(1) A wicked man has a mountain of guilt upon him, and is it easy to rise up under such a weight? Is salvation *per saltum* (obtained with a leap)? Can a man jump out of sin into heaven? Can he leap out of the devil's arms into Abraham's bosom?

(2) If all the power in a sinner be employed against repentance, then repentance is not easy. All the faculties of a natural man join issue with sin: 'I have loved strangers, and after them will I go' (*Jer.* 2.25). A sinner will rather lose Christ and heaven than his lusts. Death, which parts man and wife, will not part a wicked man and his sins; and is it so easy to repent? The angel rolled away the stone from the sepulchre, but no angel, only God himself, can roll away the stone from the heart.

3. *Presuming thoughts of God's mercy*

Many suck poison from this sweet flower. Christ who came into the world to save sinners (*1 Tim.* 1.15) is accidentally the occasion of many a man's perishing. Though to the elect he is the bread of life, yet to the wicked he is 'a stone of stumbling' (*1 Pet.* 2.8). To some his blood is sweet wine, to others the water of Marah. Some are softened by this Sun of righteousness (*Mal.* 4.2), others are hardened. Oh, says one, Christ has died; he has done all for me; therefore I may sit still and do nothing. Thus they suck death from the tree of life and perish by a saviour. So I may say of God's mercy. It is accidentally the cause of many a one's ruin. Because of mercy men presume and think they may go on in sin, but should a king's clemency make his subjects rebel? The psalmist says, there is mercy with God, that he *may be feared* (Ps. 130.4), but not that we may sin. Can men expect mercy by provoking justice? God will hardly show those mercy who sin because mercy abounds.

4. A supine sluggish temper

Repentance is looked upon as a tedious thing and such as requires much industry and men are settled upon their lees and care not to stir. They had rather go sleeping to hell than weeping to heaven. 'A slothful man hideth his hand in his bosom' (*Prov.* 19.24); he will not be at the labour of smiting on his breast. Many will rather lose heaven than ply the oar and row thither upon the waters of repentance. We cannot have the world *citra pulverem* (without labour and diligence), and would we have that which is more excellent? Sloth is the cancer of the soul: 'Slothfulness casteth into a deep sleep' (*Prov.* 19.15).

It was a witty fiction of the poets that when Mercury had cast Argus into a sleep and with an enchanted rod closed his eyes, he then killed him. When Satan has by his witcheries lulled men asleep in sloth, then he destroys them. Some report that while the crocodile sleeps with its mouth open, the Indian rat gets into its belly and eats up its entrails. So while men sleep in security they are devoured.

5. The tickling pleasure of sin: 'who had pleasure in unrighteousness' (2 Thess. 2.12)

Sin is a sugared draught, mixed with poison. The sinner thinks there is danger in sin, but there is also delight, and the danger does not terrify him as much as the delight bewitches him. Plato[1] calls love of sin a great devil.

[1] One of the greatest of Greek philosophers. He lived in the fourth century B.C.

Delighting in sin hardens the heart. In true repentance there must be a grieving for sin, but how can one grieve for that which he loves? He who delights in sin can hardly pray against it. His heart is so inveigled with sin that he is afraid of leaving it too soon. Samson doted on Delilah's beauty and her lap proved his grave. When a man rolls iniquity as a sugared lump under his tongue, it infatuates him and is his death at last. Delight in sin is a silken halter. Will it not be bitterness in the latter end (2 *Sam.* 2.26)?

6. *An opinion that repentance will take away our joy*
But that is a mistake. It does not crucify but clarify our joy, and takes it off from the fulsome lees of sin. What is all earthly joy? It is but *hilaris insania* (a pleasant frenzy). *Falsa inter gaudia noctem egerimus*[1] (Virgil). Worldly mirth is but like a feigned laugh. It has sorrow following at the heels. Like the magician's rod, it is instantly turned into a serpent; but divine repentance, like Samson's lion, has a honeycomb in it. God's kingdom consists as well in joy as in righteousness (*Rom.* 14.17). None are so truly cheerful as penitent ones. *Est quaedam flere voluptas*[2] (Ovid).

The oil of joy is poured chiefly into a broken heart: 'the oil of joy for mourning' (*Isa.* 61.3). In the fields near Palermo grow a great many reeds in which there is a sweet juice from which sugar is made. Likewise in a penitent heart, which is the bruised reed, grow the sugared joys of God's Spirit. God turns the water of tears into the juice of the grape which exhilarates and makes glad the heart. Who should rejoice if not the repenting soul? He is heir to all the promises, and is not that matter for joy? God dwells in a contrite heart, and must there not needs be joy there? 'I dwell with him that is of a

[1]'Among false joys we drive away the night.'
[2]'There is a kind of satisfaction in weeping.'

contrite spirit, to revive the heart of the contrite ones' (*Isa.* 57.15). Repentance does not take away a Christian's music, but raises it a note higher and makes it sweeter.

7. *Another obstacle to repentance is despondency of mind*

It is a vain thing for me, says the sinner, to set upon repentance; my sins are of that magnitude that there is no hope for me. 'Return ye now every one from his evil way . . . And they said, There is no hope' (*Jer. 18.11,12*). Our sins are mountains, and how shall these ever be cast into the sea? Where unbelief represents sin in its bloody colours and God in his judge's robes, the soul would sooner fly from him than to him. This is dangerous. Other sins need mercy, but despair rejects mercy. It throws the cordial of Christ's blood on the ground. Judas was not damned only for his treason and murder, but it was his distrust of God's mercy that destroyed him. Why should we entertain such hard thoughts of God? He has bowels of love to repenting sinners (*Joel 2.13*). Mercy rejoices over justice. God's anger is not so hot but mercy can cool it, nor so sharp but mercy can sweeten it. God counts his mercy his glory (*Exod. 33.18,19*). We have some drops of mercy ourselves, but God is 'the Father of mercies' (*2 Cor. 1.3*), who begets all the mercies that are in us. He is the God of tenderness and compassion. No sooner do we mourn than God's heart melts. No sooner do our tears fall than God's repentings kindle (*Hos. 11.8*). Do not say then that there is no hope. Disband the army of your sins, and God will sound a retreat to his judgments. Remember, great sins have been swallowed up in the sea of God's infinite compassions. Manasseh made the streets run with blood, yet when his head was a fountain of tears, God grew propitious.

8. *Hope of impunity*

Men flatter themselves in sin and think that God, having

spared them all this while, never intends to punish. Because the assizes are put off, therefore, surely there will be no assizes. 'He hath said in his heart, God hath forgotten: he hideth his face, he will never see it' (*Ps. 10.11*). The Lord indeed is longsuffering towards sinners and would by his patience bribe them to repentance, but here is their wretchedness; because he forbears to punish they forbear to repent. Know, that the lease of patience will soon run out. There is a time when God will say, 'My Spirit shall not always strive with man' (*Gen. 6.3*). A creditor may forbear his debtor, but forbearance does not excuse the payment. God takes notice how long the glass of his patience has been running: 'I gave her space to repent; and she repented not' (*Rev. 2.21*). Jezebel added impenitence to her incontinency, and what followed? 'Behold, I will cast her into a bed' (*Rev. 2.22*), not a bed of pleasure, but a bed of languishing where she will consume away in her iniquity. The longer God's arrow is drawing, the deeper it will wound. Sins against patience will make a man's hell so much the hotter.

9. *The next impediment of repentance is fear of reproach*

If I repent I shall expose myself to men's scorns. The heathen could say, when you apply yourself to the study of wisdom, prepare for sarcasms and reproaches. But consider well who they are that reproach you. They are such as are ignorant of God and spiritually frantic.[1] And are you troubled to have them reproach you, who are not well in their wits? Who minds a madman laughing at him?

What do the wicked reproach you for? Is it because you repent? You are doing your duty. Bind their reproaches as a crown about your head. It is better that

---

[1] Ragingly mad, delirious, insanely foolish.

men should reproach you for repenting than that God should damn you for not repenting.

If you cannot bear a reproach for religion, never call yourself Christian. Luther said, '*Christianus quasi crucianus*' (a Christian is as if a crucified one). Suffering is a saint's livery. And alas, what are reproaches? They are but chips off the cross, which are rather to be despised than laid to heart.

10. *The last impediment of repentance is immoderate love of the world*

No wonder Ezekiel's hearers were hardened into rebellion when their hearts went after covetousness (*Ezek. 33.31*). The world so engrosses men's time and bewitches their affections that they cannot repent. They had rather put gold in their bag than tears in God's bottle. I have read of the Turks that they give heed to neither churches nor altars, but are diligent in looking after their tillage. Likewise many scarcely ever give heed to repentance; they are more for the plough and breaking of clods than breaking up the fallow ground of their hearts. The thorns choke the word. We read of those who were invited to Christ's supper who put him off with worldly excuses. The first said, 'I have bought a piece of ground, and I must needs go and see it: I pray thee have me excused. And another said, I have bought five yoke of oxen . . .' (*Luke 14. 18–19*). The farm and the shop so take up people's time that they have no leisure for their souls. Their golden weights hinder their silver tears. There is an herb in the country of Sardinia, like balm, which if they eat much of, will make them die laughing. Such an herb (or rather, weed) is the world, if men eat too immoderately of it. Instead of dying repenting, they will die laughing.

These are the obstructions to repentance which must be removed so that the current may be clearer.

Chapter Eleven

PRESCRIBING SOME MEANS FOR REPENTANCE: (1) SERIOUS CONSIDERATION

In the last place I shall prescribe some rules or means conducive to repentance.

The first means conducive to repentance is serious consideration: 'I thought on my ways, and turned my feet unto thy testimonies' (*Ps. 119.59*). The prodigal, when he came to himself, seriously considered his riotous luxuries, and then he repented. Peter, when he thought of Christ's words, wept. There are certain things which, if they were well considered of, would be a means to make us break off a course of sinning.

1. Firstly, *consider seriously what sin is*, and sure enough there is enough evil in it to make us repent. There are in sin these twenty evils:

(1) Every sin is a recession from God (*Jer. 2.5*). God is the supreme good, and our blessedness lies in union with him. But sin, like a strong bias, draws away the heart from God. The sinner takes his leave of God. He bids farewell to Christ and mercy. Every step forward in sin is a step backward from God: 'they have forsaken the Lord, they are gone away backward' (*Isa. 1.4*). The further one goes from the sun, the nearer he approaches to darkness. The further the soul goes from God, the nearer it approaches to misery.

(2) Sin is a walking contrary to God (*Lev. 26.27*). The same word in the Hebrew signifies both to commit sin

and to rebel. Sin is God's opposite. If God be of one mind, sin will be of another. If God says, sanctify the Sabbath, sin says, profane it. Sin strikes at God's very being. If sin could help it, God should be no longer God: 'cause the Holy One of Israel to cease from before us' (*Isa. 30.11*). What a horrible thing is this, for a piece of proud dust to rise up in defiance against its Maker!

(3) Sin is an injury to God. It violates his laws. Here is *crimen laesae majestatis* (grievous high treason). What greater injury can be offered to a prince than to trample upon his royal edicts? A sinner offers contempt to the statute-laws of heaven: 'they cast thy law behind their backs' (*Neh. 9.26*), as if they scorned to look upon it. Sin robs God of his due. You injure a man when you do not give him his due. The soul belongs to God. He lays a double claim to it: it is his by creation and by purchase. Now sin steals the soul from God and gives the devil that which rightly belongs to God.

(4) Sin is profound ignorance. The Schoolmen say that all sin is founded in ignorance. If men knew God in his purity and justice they would not dare go on in a course of sinning: 'they proceed from evil to evil, and they know not me, saith the Lord' (*Jer. 9.3*). Therefore ignorance and lust are joined together (*1 Pet. 1.14*). Ignorance is the womb of lust. Vapours arise most in the night. The black vapours of sin arise most in a dark ignorant soul. Satan casts a mist before a sinner so that he does not see the flaming sword of God's wrath. The eagle first rolls himself in the sand and then flies at the stag, and by fluttering its wings, so bedusts the stag's eyes that it cannot see, and then it strikes it with its talons. So Satan, that eagle or prince of the air, first blinds men with ignorance and then wounds them with his darts of temptation. Is sin ignorance? There is great cause to repent of ignorance.

(5) Sin is a piece of desperateness. In every transgression a man runs an apparent hazard of his soul. He treads upon the brink of the bottomless pit. Foolish sinner, you never commit a sin but you do that which may undo your soul for ever. He who drinks poison, it is a wonder if it does not cost him his life. One taste of the forbidden tree lost Adam paradise. One sin of the angels lost them heaven. One sin of Saul lost him his kingdom. The next sin you commit God may clap you up prisoner among the damned. You who gallop on in sin, it is a question whether God will spare your life a day longer or give you a heart to repent, so that you are desperate even to frenzy.

(6) Sin besmears with filth. In James 1.21 it is called 'filthiness'. The Greek word signifies the putrid matter of ulcers. Sin is called an abomination (*Deut. 7.25*), indeed, in the plural, abominations (*Deut. 20.18*). This filthiness in sin is inward. A spot on the face may easily be wiped off, but to have the liver and lungs tainted is far worse. Such a pollution is sin, it has gotten into mind and conscience (*Titus 1.15*). It is compared to a menstruous cloth (*Isa. 30.22*), the most unclean thing under the law. A sinner's heart is like a field spread with dung. Some think sin an ornament; it is rather an excrement. Sin so besmears a person with filth that God cannot abide the sight of him: 'my soul loathed them' (*Zech. 11.8*).

(7) In sin there is odious ingratitude. God has fed you, O sinner, with angels' food. He has crowned you with a variety of mercies, yet do you go on in sin? As David said of Nabal: 'in vain have I kept this man's sheep' (*1 Sam. 25.21*). Likewise in vain has God done so much for the sinner. All God's mercies may upbraid, yea, accuse, the ungrateful person. God may say, I gave you wit, health, riches, and you have employed all these against me: 'I gave her corn, and wine, and oil, and multiplied her silver and gold, which they prepared for Baal' (*Hos. 2.8*); I sent

in provisions and they served their idols with them. The snake in the fable which was frozen stung him that brought it to the fire and gave it warmth. So a sinner goes about to sting God with his own mercies. 'Is this thy kindness to thy friend?' (*2 Sam. 16.17*). Did God give you life to sin? Did he give you wages to serve the devil?

(8) Sin is a debasing thing. It degrades a person of his honour: 'I will make thy grave; for thou art vile' (*Nah. 1.14*). This was spoken of a king. He was not vile by birth but by sin. Sin blots our name, taints our blood. Nothing so changes a man's glory into shame as sin. It is said of Naaman, 'He was a great man and honourable, but he was a leper' (*2 Kings 5.1*). Let a man be never so great with worldly pomp, yet if he be wicked he is a leper in God's eye. To boast of sin is to boast of that which is our infamy; as if a prisoner should boast of his fetters or be proud of his halter.

(9) Sin is a damage. In every sin there is infinite loss. Never did any thrive by grazing on this common. What does one lose? He loses God; he loses his peace; he loses his soul. The soul is a divine spark lighted from heaven; it is the glory of creation. And what can countervail this loss (*Matt. 16.26*)? If the soul be gone, the treasure is gone; therefore in sin there is infinite loss. Sin is such a trade that whoever follows it is sure to be ruined.

(10) Sin is a burden: 'mine iniquities are gone over mine head: as an heavy burden they are too heavy for me' (*Ps. 38.4*). The sinner goes with his weights and fetters on him. The burden of sin is always worst when it is least felt. Sin is a burden wherever it comes. Sin burdens God: 'I am pressed under you, as a cart is pressed that is full of sheaves' (*Amos 2.13*). Sin burdens the soul. What a weight did Spira[1] feel? How was the conscience of Judas

[1] See footnote on p.50

burdened, so much so that he hanged himself to quiet his conscience! They that know what sin is will repent that they carry such a burden.

(11) Sin is a debt. It is compared to a debt of ten thousand talents (*Matt. 18.24*). Of all the debts we owe, our sins are the worst. With other debts a sinner may flee to foreign parts, but with sin he cannot. 'Whither shall I flee from thy presence?' (*Ps. 139.7*). God knows where to find out all his debtors. Death frees a man from other debts but it will not free him from this. It is not the death of the debtor but of the creditor that discharges this debt.

(12) There is deceitfulness in sin (*Heb. 3.13*). 'The wicked worketh a deceitful work' (*Prov. 11.18*). Sin is a mere cheat. While it pretends to please us, it beguiles us! Sin does as Jael did. First she brought the milk and butter to Sisera, then she struck the nail through his temples so that he died (*Judg. 5.26*). Sin first courts, and then kills. It is first a fox and then a lion. Whoever sin kills it betrays. Those locusts in the Revelation are the perfect hieroglyphics and emblems of sin: 'on their heads were as it were crowns like gold, and they had hair as the hair of women, and their teeth were as the teeth of lions, and there were stings in their tails' (*Rev. 9.7–10*). Sin is like the usurer who feeds a man with money and then makes him mortgage his land. Sin feeds the sinner with delightful objects and then makes him mortgage his soul. Judas pleased himself with the thirty pieces of silver, but they proved deceitful riches. Ask him now how he likes his bargain.

(13) Sin is a spiritual sickness. One man is sick of pride, another of lust, another of malice. It is with a sinner as it is with a sick patient: his palate is distempered, and the sweetest things taste bitter to him. So the word of God, which is sweeter than the honeycomb, tastes bitter to a sinner: 'They put sweet for bitter' (*Isa.*

5.20). And if sin be a disease it is not to be cherished, but rather cured by repentance.

(14) Sin is a bondage. It binds a man apprentice to the devil. Of all conditions, servitude is the worst. Every man is held with the cords of his own sin. I was held before conversion, said Augustine, not with an iron chain, but with the obstinacy of my will. Sin is imperious and tyrannical. It is called a law (*Rom. 8.2*) because it has such a binding power over a man. The sinner must do as sin will have him. He does not so much enjoy his lusts as serve them, and he will have work enough to do to gratify them all. 'I have seen princes going on foot' (*Eccles. 10.7*); the soul, that princely thing, which did once sit in a chair of state and was crowned with knowledge and holiness, is now made a lackey to sin and runs the devil's errand.

(15) Sin has a spreading malignity in it. It does hurt not only to a man's self, but to others. One man's sin may occasion many to sin, as one beacon being lighted may occasion all the beacons in the country to be lighted. One man may help to defile many. A person who has the plague, going into company, does not know how many will be infected with the plague by him. You who are guilty of open sins know not how many have been infected by you. There may be many, for ought you know, now in hell, crying out that they would never have come thither if it had not been for your bad example.

(16) Sin is a vexatious thing. It brings trouble with it. The curse which God laid upon the woman is most truly laid upon every sinner: 'in sorrow thou shalt bring forth' (*Gen. 3.16*). A man vexes his thoughts with plotting sin, and when sin has conceived, in sorrow he brings forth. Like one who takes a great deal of pain to open a floodgate, when he has opened it, the flood comes in upon him and drowns him. So a man beats his brains to contrive

sin, and then it vexes his conscience, brings crosses to his estate, rots the wall and timber of his house (*Zech. 5.4*).

(17) Sin is an absurd thing. What greater indiscretion is there than to gratify an enemy? Sin gratifies Satan. When lust or anger burn in the soul, Satan warms himself at the fire. Men's sins feast the devil. Samson was called out to make the lords of the Philistines sport (*Judg. 16.25*). Likewise the sinner makes the devil sport. It is meat and drink to him to see men sin. How he laughs to see them venturing their souls for the world, as if one should venture diamonds for straws, or should fish for gudgeons with golden hooks. Every wicked man shall be indicted for a fool at the day of judgment.

(18) There is cruelty in every sin. With every sin you commit, you give a stab to your soul. While you are kind to sin you are cruel to yourself, like the man in the Gospel who cut himself with stones till the blood came (*Mark 5.5*). The sinner is like the jailer who drew a sword to kill himself (*Acts 16.27*). The soul may cry out, I am murdering. Naturalists say the hawk chooses to drink blood rather than water. So sin drinks the blood of souls.

(19) Sin is a spiritual death: 'dead in trespasses and INS' (*Eph. 2.1*). Augustine said that before his conversion, reading of the death of Dido,¹ he could not refrain from weeping. But wretch that I was, said he, I bewailed the death of Dido forsaken of Aeneas and did not bewail the death of my soul forsaken of God. The life of sin is the death of the soul.

A dead man has no sense. So an unregenerate person has no sense of God in him (*Eph. 4.19*). Persuade him to mind his salvation? To what purpose do you make orations to a dead man? Go to reprove him for vice? To what purpose do you strike a dead man?

¹The legendary founder of Carthage who stabbed herself to death because she could not obtain Aeneas as a husband (tenth century B.C.).

He who is dead has no taste. Set a banquet before him, and he does not relish it. Likewise a sinner tastes no sweetness in Christ or a promise. They are but as cordials in a dead man's mouth.

The dead putrify; and if Martha said of Lazarus, 'Lord, by this time he stinketh: for he hath been dead four days' (*John 11.39*), how much more may we say of a wicked man, who has been dead in sin for thirty or forty years, 'by this time he stinketh'!

(20) Sin without repentance tends to final damnation. As the rose perishes by the canker bred in itself, so do men by the corruptions which breed in their souls. What was once said to the Grecians of the Trojan horse,[1] This engine is made to be the destruction of your city, the same may be said to every impenitent person, 'This engine of sin will be the destruction of your soul'. Sin's last scene is always tragic. Diagoras Florentinus would drink poison in a frolic, but it cost him his life. Men drink the poison of sin in a merriment, but it costs them their souls: 'the wages of sin is death' (*Rom. 6.23*). What Solomon said of wine may also be said of sin: at first 'it giveth his colour in the cup. At the last it biteth like a serpent, and stingeth like an adder' (*Prov. 23.31–2*). Christ tell us of the worm and the fire (*Mark 9.48*). Sin is like oil, and God's wrath is like fire. As long as the damned continue sinning, so the fire will continue scorching, and 'who among us shall dwell with everlasting burnings?' (*Isa. 33.14*). But men question the truth of this and are like impious Devonax who, being threatened with hell for his villainies, mocked at it and said, I will believe there is a hell when I come there, and not before. We cannot make hell enter into men till they enter into hell.

Thus we have seen the deadly evil in sin which,

[1]See footnote on p. 51

seriously considered, may make us repent and turn to God. If, for all this, men will persist in sin and are resolved upon a voyage to hell, who can help it? They have been told what a soul-damning rock sin is, but if they will voluntarily run upon it and split themselves, their blood be upon their own head.

2. *The second serious consideration to work repentance is to consider the mercies of God.*

A stone is soonest broken upon a soft pillow, and a heart of stone is soonest broken upon the soft pillow of God's mercies: 'the goodness of God leadeth thee to repentance' (*Rom.* 2.4). The clemency of a prince sooner causes relenting in a malefactor. While God has been storming others by his judgments he has been wooing you by his mercies.

(1) What private mercies have we had? What mischiefs have been prevented, what fears blown over? When our foot has been slipping, God's mercy has held us up (*Ps. 94.18*). Mercy has always been a screen between us and danger. When enemies like lions have risen up against us to devour us, free grace has snatched us out of the mouth of these lions. In the deepest waves the arm of mercy has been under and has kept our head above water. And will not this privative mercy lead us to repentance?

(2) What positive mercies have we had! Firstly, in supplying mercy. God has been a bountiful benefactor: 'the God which fed me all my life long unto this day' (*Gen. 48.15*). What man will spread a table for his enemy? We have been enemies, yet God has fed us. He has given us the horn of oil. He has made the honeycomb of mercy drop on us. God has been as kind to us as if we had been his best servants. And will not this supplying mercy lead us to repentance? Secondly, in delivering mercy. When we have been at the gates of the grave, God

has miraculously spun out our lives. He has turned the shadow of death into morning and has put a song of deliverance into our mouth. And will not delivering mercy lead us to repentance? The Lord has laboured to break our hearts with his mercies. In Judges, chapter 2, we read that when the angel (which was a prophet) had preached a sermon of mercy, 'the people lifted up their voice, and wept' (*v. 4*). If anything will move tears, it should be the mercy of God. He is an obstinate sinner indeed whom these great cable-ropes of God's mercy will not draw to repentance.

3. *In the third place, consider God's afflictive providences,* and see if our limbeck[1] will not drop when the fire is put under. God has sent us in recent years to the school of the cross. He has twisted his judgments together. He has made good upon us those two threatenings, 'I will be to Ephraim as a moth' (*Hos. 5.12*) – has not God been so to England in the decay of trading? – and 'I will be unto Ephraim as a lion' (*Hos. 5.14*) – has he not been so to England in the devouring plague?[2] All this while God waited for our repentance. But we went on in sin: 'I hearkened and heard, but no man repented him of his wickedness, saying, What have I done?' (*Jer. 8.6*). And of late God has been whipping us with a fiery rod in those tremendous flames in this city,[3] which were emblematic of the great conflagration at the last day when 'the elements shall melt with fervent heat' (*2 Pet. 3.10*). When Joab's corn was on fire, then he went running to Absalom (*2 Sam. 14.31*). God has set our houses on fire that we may run to him in repentance. 'The Lord's voice crieth unto the city: hear ye the rod, and who hath appointed it' (*Mic. 6.9*). This is the language of the rod, that we should

[1]See foot note on p. 19
[2]The plague of 1665.
[3]The Great Fire of London in 1666.

humble ourselves under God's mighty hand and 'break off our sins by righteousness' (*Dan.* 4.27). Manasseh's affliction ushered in repentance (2 *Chron.* 33.12). This God uses as the proper medicine for security. 'Their mother hath played the harlot' (*Hos.* 2.5), by idolatry. What course now will God take with her? 'Therefore I will hedge up thy way with thorns' (*Hos.* 2.6). This is God's method, to set a thorn-hedge of affliction in the way. Thus to a proud man contempt is a thorn. To a lustful man sickness is a thorn, both to stop him in his sin and to prick him forward in repentance.

The Lord teaches his people as Gideon did the men of Succoth: 'He took the elders of the city, and thorns of the wilderness and briers, and with them he taught the men of Succoth' (*Judg.* 8.16). Here was tearing rhetoric. Likewise God has of late been teaching us humiliation by thorny providences. He has torn our golden fleece from us; he has brought our houses low that he might bring our hearts low. When shall we dissolve into tears if not now? God's judgments are so proper a means to work repentance that the Lord wonders at it, and makes it his complaint that his severity did not break men off from their sins: 'I have with-holden the rain from you' (*Amos* 4.7); 'I have smitten you with blasting and mildew' (*Amos* 4.9); 'I have sent among you the pestilence' (*Amos* 4.10). But still this is the burden of the complaint, 'Yet ye have not returned to me'.

The Lord proceeds gradually in his judgments. Firstly, he sends a lesser cross, and if that will not do, then a greater. He sends upon one a gentle fit of an ague to begin with, and afterwards a burning fever. He sends upon another a loss at sea, then the loss of a child, then of a husband. Thus by degrees he tries to bring men to repentance.

Sometimes God makes his judgments go in circuit,

from family to family. The cup of affliction has gone round the nation; all have tasted it. And if we repent not now, we stand in contempt of God, and by implication we bid God do his worst. Such a climax of wickedness will hardly be pardoned. 'In that day did the Lord God of hosts call to weeping, and to mourning . . . And behold joy and gladness . . . And it was revealed in mine ears by the Lord of hosts, Surely this iniquity shall not be purged from you till you die' (*Isa.* 22.12–14). That is, this sin shall not be expiated by sacrifice.

If the Romans severely punished a young man who in a time of public calamity was seen sporting in a window with a crown of roses on his head, of how much sorer punishment shall they be thought worthy who strengthen themselves in wickedness and laugh in the very face of God's judgments. The heathen mariners in a storm repented (*Jon* 1.14). Not to repent now and throw our sins overboard is to be worse than heathens.

4. *Fourthly, let us consider how much we shall have to answer for at last if we repent not,* how many prayers, counsels, and admonitions will be put upon the score. Every sermon will come in as an indictment. As for such as have truly repented, Christ will answer for them. His blood will wash away their sins. The mantle of free grace will cover them. 'In those days, saith the Lord, the iniquity of Israel shall be sought for, and there shall be none; and the sins of Judah, and they shall not be found' (*Jer.* 50.20). Those who have judged themselves in the lower court of conscience shall be acquitted in the High Court of heaven. But if we repent not, our sins must be all accounted for at the last day, and we must answer for them in our own persons, with no counsel allowed to plead for us.

O impenitent sinner, think with yourself now how you will be able to look your judge in the face. You have a damned cause to plead and will be sure to be cast at the bar[1]: 'What then shall I do when God riseth up? and when he visiteth, what shall I answer him?' (*Job 31.14*). Therefore, either repent now, or else provide your answers and see what defence you can make for yourselves when you come before God's tribunal. But when God rises up, how will you answer him?

[1] Rejected at the bar of judgment.

Chapter Twelve

PRESCRIBING SOME MEANS FOR REPENTANCE: (2) COMPARE PENITENT AND IMPENITENT CONDITIONS

The second help to repentance is a prudent comparison. Compare penitent and impenitent conditions together and see the difference. Spread them before your eyes and by the light of the word see the impenitent condition as most deplorable and the penitent as most comfortable. How sad was it with the prodigal before he returned to his father! He had spent all; he had sinned himself into beggary, and had nothing left but a few husks. He was fellow-commoner with the swine, but when he came home to his father, nothing was thought too good for him. The robe was brought forth to cover him, the ring to adorn him, and the fatted calf to feast him. If the sinner continues in his impenitency, then farewell Christ and mercy. But if he repent, then presently he has a heaven within him. Then Christ is his, then all is peace. He may sing a requiem to his soul and say, 'Soul, take thine ease, thou hast much goods laid up' (*Luke 12.19*). Upon our turning to God we have more restored to us in Christ than ever was lost in Adam. God says to the repenting soul, I will clothe thee with the robe of righteousness; I will enrich thee with the jewels and graces of my Spirit. I will bestow my love upon thee; I will give thee a kingdom: 'Son, all I have is thine'. O my friends, do but compare your estate before repentance and after repentance together. Before your repenting, there are nothing but clouds to be seen and storms, clouds in God's face and storms in conscience. But after repenting how is the weather altered! What sunshine above! What serene calmness within! A Christian's soul being like the hill Olympus,[1] all light and clear, and no winds blowing.

A third means conducive to repentance is a settled determination to leave sin. Not a faint velleity, but a resolved vow. 'I have sworn that I will keep thy righteous judgments' (*Ps. 119.106*). All the delights and artifices of sin shall not make me forsworn. There must be no hesitation, no consulting with flesh and blood, Had I best leave my sin or no? But as Ephraim, 'What have I to do any more with idols?' (*Hos. 14.8*). I will be gulled no more by my sins, no longer fooled by Satan. This day I will put a bill of divorce into the hands of my lusts. Till we come to this peremptory resolution, sin will get ground of us and we shall never be able to shake off this viper. It is no wonder that he who is not resolved to be an enemy of sin is conquered by it.

But this resolution must be built upon the strength of Christ more than our own. It must be a humble resolution. As David, when he went against Goliath put off his presumptuous confidence as well as his armour – 'I come to thee in the name of the Lord' (*1 Sam. 17.45*) – so we must go out against our Goliath-lusts in the strength of Christ. It is usual for a person to join another in the bond with him. So, being conscious of our own inability to leave sin, let us get Christ to be bound with us and engage his strength for the mortifying of corruption.

The fourth means conducive to repentance is earnest supplication. The heathens laid one of their hands on the plough, the other they lifted up to Ceres, the goddess of

[1] In Greek mythology, the home of the gods.

corn. So when we have used the means, let us look up to God for a blessing. Pray to him for a repenting heart: 'Thou, Lord, who bidst me repent, give me grace to repent'. Pray that our hearts may be holy limbecks dropping tears. Beg of Christ to give to us such a look of love as he did to Peter, which made him go out and weep bitterly. Implore the help of God's Spirit. It is the Spirit's smiting on the rock of our hearts that makes the waters gush out: 'He causes his wind to blow and the waters flow' (*Ps. 147.18*). When the wind of God's Spirit blows, then the water of tears will flow.

There is good reason we should to God for repentance:

(1) Because it is his gift: 'Then hath God also to the Gentiles granted repentance unto life' (*Acts 11.18*). The Arminians hold that it is in our power to repent. We can harden our hearts, but we cannot soften them. This crown of free-will is fallen from our head. Nay, there is in us not only impotency, but obstinacy (*Acts 7.51*). Therefore beg of God a repentant spirit. He can make the stony heart bleed. His is a word of creative power.

(2) We must have recourse to God for blessing because he has promised to bestow it: 'I will give you an heart of flesh' (*Ezek. 36.26*). I will soften your adamant hearts in my Son's blood. Show God his hand and seal. And there is another gracious promise: 'They shall return unto me with their whole heart' (*Jer. 24.7*). Turn this promise into a prayer: Lord, give me grace to return unto thee with my whole heart.

The fifth means conducive to repentance is endeavour after clearer discoveries of God: 'Now mine eye seeth thee. Wherefore I abhor myself, and repent in dust and ashes' (*Job 42.5–6*). Job, having surveyed God's glory and purity, as a humble penitent did abhor, or as it is in the Hebrew, did even reprobate, himself. By looking into the transparent glass of God's holiness, we see our own blemishes and so learn to bewail them.

Lastly, we should labour for faith. But what is that to repentance? Yes, faith breeds union with Christ, and there can be no separation from sin till there be union with Christ. The eye of faith looks on mercy and that thaws the heart. Faith carries us to Christ's blood, and that blood mollifies. Faith persuades of the love of God, and that love sets us a-weeping.

Thus I have laid down the means or helps to repentance. What remains now but that we set upon the work. And let us be in earnest, not as fencers but as warriors.

I will conclude all with the words of the psalmist: 'He that goeth forth and weepeth, bearing precious seed, shall doubtless come again with rejoicing, bringing his sheaves with him' (*Ps. 126.6*).

SOME OTHER
THOMAS WATSON
TITLES
BY
BANNER OF TRUTH

A BODY OF DIVINITY
Thomas Watson

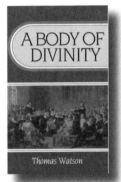

The first book published by the Trust, this has been one of the best sellers and consistently the most useful and influential of our publications. There are several reasons for this:

1. *The subject of the book.* It deals with the foremost doctrinal and experimental truths of the Christian Faith.

2. *The means of instruction used.* It is based on the Westminster Assembly's *Shorter Catechism*, in which the main principles of Christianity that lie scattered in the Scriptures are brought together and set forth in the form of question and answer. This Catechism is unsurpassed for its 'terse exactitude of definition' and 'logical elaboration' of the fundamentals.

3. *The style of the author.* Watson conveys his thorough doctrinal and experimental knowledge of the truth in such an original, concise, pithy, pungent, racy, rich and illustrative style that he is rightly regarded as the most readable of the Puritans.

ISBN 978 0 85151 383 6
328pp.   Large paperback

THE TEN COMMANDMENTS
Thomas Watson

In this book Thomas Watson (c.1620-
1686) continues his exposition of the
Shorter Catechism drawn up by the
Westminster Assembly. Watson was
one of the most popular preachers in
London during the Puritan era. His
writings are characterised by clarity,
raciness and spiritual richness. The
series of three volumes, of which this
is the second, makes an ideal introduction to Puritan literature.

There are few matters about which the Puritans differ
more from present-day Christians than in their assess-
ment of the importance of the ten commandments. The
commandments, they held, are the first thing in Christianity which the natural man needs to be taught and they
should be the daily concern of the Christian to the last.

In *The Ten Commandments* Watson examines the moral
law as a whole as well as bringing out the meaning and
force of each particular commandment. In view of the
most important function of the law in Christian life and
evangelism this is a most valuable volume.

ISBN 978 0 85151 146 7
288pp.   Large paperback

THE LORD'S PRAYER
Thomas Watson

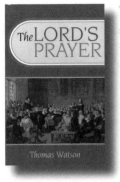

Thomas Watson's clarity, raciness and spiritual richness of writing are nowhere seen so clearly as in his outstandingly helpful exposition of the *Shorter Catechism* drawn up by the Westminster Assembly. The three-volume edition (of which this is the third) makes an ideal guide to Christian doctrine and practice and also serves as a wonderful introduction to Puritan literature.

In *The Lord's Prayer* Watson analyses in detail the preface to the prayer and thre six petitions which it contains. His treatment of the words 'thy kingdom come' is exceptionally full, illuminating and stirring. Like all great books on prayer, it provides practical help because it concentrates on biblical instruaction.

ISBN 978 0 85151 145 0
344pp. Large paperback

ALL THINGS FOR GOOD

Thomas Watson

Thomas Watson of St. Stephen's, Wal-
brook believed he faced two great dif-
ficulties in his pastoral ministry. The
first was making the unbeliever sad,
in the recognition of his need of God's
grace. The second was making the
believer joyful in response to God's
grace. He believed the answer to the
second difficulty could be found in
Paul's teaching in Romans 8.28: God
works all things together for good for his people.

Watson's exposition is always simple, illuminating and
rich in practical application. He explains that both the
best and the worst experiences work for the good of
God's people. He carefully analyses what it means to be
someone who 'loves God' and is 'called according to his
purpose'. *All Things For Good* provides the biblical answer to the contemporary question: 'Why do bad things
happen to good people?'

ISBN 978 0 85151 478 9
128pp. Paperback

For more information about our publications, or to order,
please visit our website.

THE BANNER OF TRUTH TRUST

3 Murrayfield Road, P O Box 621, Carlisle,
Edinburgh EH12 6EL PA 17013,
UK USA
www.banneroftruth.co.uk